D0423731

to deeply loved, Kim Anthony has lived an extraordinary life and invites all of us to share in the hope-filled highlights.

—Gary Thomas, author of
*Sacred Marriage* and *Pure Pleasure*

The transparency by which Kim recalls the hardships of her life allows us to experience a spectrum of emotions. It is a truly inspirational story of how faith takes her from abandonment, adversity, and insecurity to forgiveness, love, and purpose.

—Ruth Riley, Olympic gold medalist, WNBA Silver Stars

Kim's story of perseverance, hard work, and faithfulness will inspire everyone. Coming from humble beginnings myself, it's amazing to hear how Kim overcame so many things and emotions to climb to the top. She is a true inspiration!

—Swin Cash, Olympic gold medalist,
WNBA Seattle Storm

No matter if you come from the Bottom or the top, God gives passion, potential, and purpose to us all. Kim's story is a testimony that God can take what most see as setbacks and turn them into setups for one's success.

—Annett Davis, 2000 Olympian, beach volleyball

Kim has outdone herself with a message that gives hope to those with less than the ideal circumstances, proving anything is possible if you work toward it. This book can inspire anyone struggling with their self-confidence, giving them the courage to step outside of their current environment and grow through life's experiences. *Unfavorable Odds* also demonstrates how God will strategically place the right people in your life at just the right time, allowing you to excel beyond belief through a relationship with him.

—Lauryn Williams, track and field world champion and Olympian

Kim scores a perfect 10! *Unfavorable Odds* is a wonderful story of trial to triumph. A timely message of hope for anyone who is going through a challenging season of life. Kim shares a transparent heart that is both candid and clear. God has a plan and purpose for us all; we just have to believe it!

—Byron Davis, former swimming world record holder

Kim Hamilton Anthony shattered the socially accepted prejudice that all great gymnasts are short and that all black gymnasts are bulky and don't have good lines. The fact that Kimmy was 5'7", stunningly beautiful, and the perfect combination of strength and grace made her an anomaly.

—Valorie Kondos Field, UCLA Gymnastics head coach

Kim's story is encouraging and inspiring. She shares how the Lord has seen her through life's difficulties. I appreciate Kim's authenticity. I know it to be true in her life as well as this book. Let the pages speak to your heart as they did to mine.

—Dr. René D. Rochester, CEO Urban S.E.T. Inc

Within these pages are penned the heart of a woman transformed by life's challenges. *Unfavorable Odds* is a very compelling and personal story of a journey taken on a road of vulnerability, personal sacrifices, and belief, ultimately, in the power of the Creator to make crooked paths straight. Contained herein also lay invitations for self-reflection and opportunities to discover lessons that are frequently hidden in life's everyday ups and downs.

—William D. Parham, PhD, ABPP, psychologist

Coach Geoff,
All the Best to you!

Kim Anthony

# UNFAVORABLE
# ODDS

The Story

Of an Unlikely

Champion

# UNFAVORABLE
# ODDS

KIM HAMILTON ANTHONY

*Cover design by Kandi Evans*
*Interior design by Stephanie Woloszyn*
*Edited by Kevin Miller*

Published in the United States of America

ISBN: 978-1-4675-9272-7
1. Biography & Autobiography / Personal Memoirs
2. Biography & Autobiography / Sports
09.11.17

## KHARI AND CALEB,

I hope you will take my life lessons and
apply them to your own.
You will never know just how much
you both mean to me.
I love you with all my heart.

## MOMMY

# ACKNOWLEDGMENTS

I want to thank my husband, Corwin, who has strongly encouraged me for years to put my story in writing. It has been a long journey. Thank you for nudging me every time I felt like giving up, and for helping me grow and heal through the process. I'm so grateful for the numerous hours you put in to help me along the way. I could not have done it without you.

Momma, words cannot express how grateful I am for all that you have done for me. Thank you for always being there. You were my strength when I was weak, my courage when I was afraid, and my faith when I didn't believe. You sacrificed daily so I could pursue my dreams. You constantly told me God wasn't through with me yet. And I believed you. You are the best mommy in the world, and I'm glad God made me *your* child. I love you more than words can say.

Daddy, without you I could not be the person I am today. Thank you for your love and support. It means so much for me to have you be a part of my life. Thanks also for giving me permission to write this book. You are a strong man, and I am so proud of you. I am glad you are my daddy, and I wouldn't change that for the world! I'll love you always.

Mike and Eldra Bunkley, you have been extremely instrumental in my spiritual growth, and I thank you for your unending encouragement and support.

As I've worked to publish this book, there have been several wonderful people who have come alongside me with tremendous support. Josh and Natalie McCown, Arlene DeBardelaben, Walt and Jamie Harber, Sharon Gamble, Dee Dee Foster Worley, and Kendra Bailey Morris, thank you for your selfless support and believing that this book could have a positive impact on the lives of others.

Shaunti Feldhahn, Chris Riley, Dr. Rene Rochester, Gary Thomas, Lesley Visser, Valorie Kondos-Field, Dr. William Parham, Swin Cash, Ruth Riley, Lauryn Williams, and Byron and Annett Davis, thank you for your kind words and your support of this book. You all have been a tremendous inspiration to me, and I count it an honor to have had you review my book.

Thank you, Robin V. Lynch, for always loving me just as I am.

I am grateful for my group of trusted friends, the Wednesday Wonders: Arlene DeBardelaben, Paulette Dawanyi, Pam Haith, Andrea Ivory, Terri Prestage-White, Chris Riley, Ruth Riley, Jenny Boucek, Sandy

Brondello, Swin Cash, and Lauryn Williams. You have walked with me through the best and worst of times and encouraged me to no end. Every woman should have a group of friends who are as special to her as you all are to me. You inspire me. Love you much!

To my family and friends in Richmond, who encouraged me, weathered snowstorms and long drives to watch me compete, and supported endless sales of cartwheels and grapefruit to help me raise money, you'll never know just how much you impacted my life. Thank you.

To all of my past UCLA family: Jerry Tomlinson, Valorie Kondos-Field, Scott Bull, Mike Vossen, Susan Armstrong, Lorita Granger, Tanya Service Chaplin, Jill Andrews-Sprague, and all of my teammates: thank you for boosting my confidence and caring for my mind, my body, and my soul. I am forever grateful to you.

To all of my past Richmond Olympiad family, Gordon and Judy Shaw, Jim Roe, Monica Manns, Dana Garber Miller, Keith, and all of my teammates with whom I grew up: thank you for your enormous support and great friendships.

A big thank you goes out to my editor, Kevin Miller, for helping me to grow as an author and making my story come alive by encouraging me to dig deeper and answer the tough questions.

Lastly, but always first in my life, I thank my God, in whom all things are possible. I could never live without your love, mercy, and forgiveness. I deserve none of it, but you continue to give it freely. I pray this book brings honor to you.

# CONTENTS

Foreword ................................................................. 17

Introduction: How Did It Come to This? ..................... 21

Where It All Began .................................................. 25

Making Daddy Happy .............................................. 33

Gymnastics? Girl, Please! ......................................... 45

Little Black Girl in a White Girl's World ..................... 53

Gotta Dance! .......................................................... 67

Funding the Dream .................................................. 73

Olympic Hopeful ..................................................... 87

Twenty-Four Magical Hours in New York .................... 91

Olympic Trials ... And Tribulations ............................ 97

The Awakening ....................................................... 105

Back to Reality ....................................................... 119

Photographs .......................................................... 127

College? Me? ......................................................... 149

A New Life Begins .................................................. 155

My "Borrowed" Family ............................................ 173

A Girl Has Got to Eat! ............................................ 179

Hard Work Pays Off ................................................ 183

Home Sweet Home? ................................................ 191

Finally, Some Answers! ........................................... 199

Defending the Title ................................................. 213

Choosing Grace ..................................................... 227

The Honor Is Mine .................................................. 245

Reconciled ............................................................ 251

Conclusion: A Beautiful Hope ................................... 257

Seven Steps from Pain to Purpose ............................ 269

# FOREWORD

Through our involvement with the National Football League, we have gotten to know Kim Anthony quite well, and she is truly a remarkable person. Kim is married to Corwin Anthony, Chaplain for the Miami Dolphins and National Director of Pro Ministries for Athletes In Action. Because the Anthonys were so involved with our players and staff, we've attended many NFL events with them over the years—chapel services at Dolphins games, NFL owners meetings, Super Bowl breakfasts, and other events. Our friendship with the Anthonys has grown primarily because of our mutual interests.

From the first day we were introduced, Kim had that special glow that attracts people to her. She is very attractive, friendly, and outgoing, but it is her inner spirit that really stands out. She is polished and articulate and always seems at ease with everyone. In short, the Kim Anthony that we came to know seemed to have it all together, all the time.

In reading *Unfavorable Odds*, however, we were introduced to Kim Hamilton, the girl who would grow to become Kim Anthony. Her story is riveting and compelling. We could have never imagined the things Kim has been through and the challenges she has experienced. She speaks openly of living in a home where her dad was in and out of her life, offering very little stability. She describes growing up with meager resources in Richmond, Virginia, living without the material comforts most of us take for granted, and having to deal with the myriad of issues confronting a young girl in that environment.

Kim also details her unlikely journey from sidewalk acrobat to world-class gymnast and the inner tensions that developed along the way. After growing up in an all black neighborhood, she had to adapt to traveling in an affluent, mostly white world while receiving criticism from her old friends that perhaps she was changing and abandoning her roots. As if that weren't enough, she was learning about athletic pressure—the physical and mental demands of training to compete at an Olympic level while trying to maintain good grades through high school and college.

As a maturing, young woman, Kim was also searching to find herself, not only physically but also emotionally and spiritually. There was pressure to maintain a "gymnast's body," one that would appeal to the media and the judges rather than one that was natural for her. She was also learning about college life, relationships, and what it's like living in the public eye. There was a lot going on in Kim Hamilton's world, enough that it certainly could have derailed her career and her life.

But this is not a book that is merely about problems, setbacks, and tough times in life. The exciting thing about this story is that Kim's experiences provide *answers*. She talks passionately about finally finding her identity and security. She shows how she overcame some huge obstacles and how she won the battle against low self-esteem not by what *she* did but by whom she trusted.

Having met Kim when she was an adult and not knowing her life story, we marvel at how she grew up and what she has accomplished. In retrospect, you can certainly see God's hands at work in shaping and molding her. As parents, and also as concerned adults who are involved in shaping our next generation, it is so encouraging to read her story and realize that there is really no limit to what any of our children can grow to become. Kim Hamilton Anthony's story is truly inspirational. It gives us all hope that no matter where we start from, no matter what adversity we have to work through, it is possible to succeed in life with hard work and determination. But, more importantly, she also shows that the best way to overcome life's challenges and issues is through discovering your identity with God.

Thank you, Kim, for having the courage to share your life so openly in this book. We know it will be a blessing to people of all ages and genders, and especially to those who are dealing with issues of identity and self-esteem.

*—Tony and Lauren Dungy*

# INTRODUCTION:

## HOW DID IT COME TO THIS?

The pain shot up my back, through my neck, and into my head. Every breath I took exited my lungs with a groan. I tried to compensate by taking small, short breaths that didn't require my rib cage to expand as much, but the pain was still excruciating. Even so, I didn't want to take my painkillers just yet. The meet didn't start for another couple of hours, and if I waited until warm-ups, there was a chance I'd make it through the entire competition with minimal discomfort.

I stared down at the hotel room bed. It was covered with media guides, photographs, note cards, and sheets of paper filled with my scribbled handwriting. It was evidence of the extensive research I had done in preparation to do color commentary for yet another gymnastics meet, this time in Athens, Georgia. As I looked at the dozens of smiling young girls with ponytails bobbing atop bodies that combined the strength of a bodybuilder with grace and unmatched athleticism, I wondered if ten years from now they would feel the same type of pain I was experiencing, the result of numerous neck and back injuries received when I was the one being studied by television commentators.

A tray of partially eaten food from room service sat on the desk. It had always been difficult for me to eat on the day of a competition. Even though I wasn't the one competing this time, this day was no different. Right before I left, I planned to force down an energy bar to ensure I had enough nutrients to keep my brain from shutting down midway through the event. I knew that once things got underway I would calm down and my appetite would return with a vengeance. So I always kept an emergency stash of crackers or some other kind of snack on hand, just in case.

As part of my pre-broadcast routine, I read the hotel's complimentary newspaper out loud. That was how I warmed up my voice, how I got the kinks out—or should I say how I got the Ebonics out? It was always easier and more comfortable for me to use slang and partial words rather than Standard English terms. But now I was in a world where I was expected to be articulate, to represent "my people" well. At the same time, I knew some would think I was a sellout for speaking proper English and that I was "trying to be white." But I refused to believe that how I spoke changed who I was. It was just a matter of communicating in a way that helped me connect with my target audience. Inside, I was still the same old Kim.

Feeling confident that I knew enough about these athletes to give some knowledgeable analysis, I turned to aesthetics—hair and makeup. The goal was to look good enough to be on camera without appearing too glamorous. I knew my play-by-play guy would only shoot from the left, so I hoped the "camera side" of my face was blemish free. I would also have to go directly from wearing a headset to doing an on-camera interview, so I had to style my hair in such a way that I could make the transition without looking as though I had just crawled out of bed.

I looked toward the bathroom, where my transformation was about to take place. The hotel room wasn't large, but the bathroom seemed so far away. I knew I would have to endure even more pain if I stood up and walked toward it, so I slid off the bed and crawled instead. Doing so brought back memories from my college years. I had injured my ankles so many times that every morning I had to crawl into the bathroom because it was too painful to walk. Then I would slowly work my way into a standing position and limp around until my joints warmed up. It took almost a year after I stopped competing before I could get out of bed like a normal person. My crippling back pain was a constant reminder of the extremes to which I had pushed myself.

After muscling my way to the vanity, I let out a sigh and waited for the pain to subside so I could sit. After a few moments, I struggled to lift my body upright, only to have the pain shoot through me again. As I waited for it to calm down, I stared at my reflection in the mirror and wondered, *Was it worth it?*

# ONE

# WHERE IT ALL BEGAN

I was destined for a rough life even before I was born. It was 1967. My mother was just a teenager when she became pregnant with me. She lived in a poor area of Richmond, Virginia. Three generations shared two bedrooms in a four-room house on South Lombardy Street. Up to thirteen people lived there at any given time. The bathroom was an outhouse located in the remote end of the backyard. When her family needed water, they had to draw it from an outdoor spigot and carry it inside. They bathed once a week in a tub in the middle of the kitchen floor. To say it was rustic would be a considerable understatement.

My mother was the youngest of five children. Her mother, my Grandma Justine, worked hard to provide for her family. She took the bus every day to labor as a maid for rich, white families. Grandpa Ben was a gravedigger. He prided himself on being the only digger who knew how to read the cemetery blueprints. Often, he would take my mother, whom he called "Baby Daughter," to the cemetery to show off his handiwork. Momma hated going there, but she didn't want to disappoint her father. As they walked among the tombstones, he would explain how the holes had to be dug in just the right shape with just the right amount of space between them. What most people would have considered a menial job gave Grandpa Ben a tremendous sense of pride and accomplishment.

However, Grandpa's work ethic was often undercut by his addiction to alcohol. His habit was no secret. When he ran out of money to buy drinks, he sat on the porch and hollered at people as they passed by on their way to the bootlegger down the street. Sometimes he was able to convince them to take him along. Then he would stagger back hours later, working his way from porch to porch, occasionally stopping in his swaying stance to judge the distance to his house.

When he finally made it home, he would pass out wherever was most convenient. Seeing as this usually happened on Friday nights, my mother's and my aunt's dates would often have to step over Grandpa Ben as he snored in the front hall. At other times they would have to sit and visit with their dates while he lay unconscious in the middle of the living room. After a while my aunt began dragging him into the kitchen before her date arrived to spare her the embarrassment. Life may not have been perfect, but it definitely was not dull!

When my mother discovered she was pregnant with me, she was in her senior year of high school. She and my father had known each other since they were thirteen years old. He was her first love, and she was his.

Daddy didn't get off to a good start in school. My grandfather was in the military and served overseas in France. Daddy was six when his family moved back to the United States. French was my father's first lan-

guage, so when he began school in America, he didn't
understand a word of English. Even after his school
assigned him a French-speaking tutor, he still had difficulty because his tutor's French was quite different from
the French he had learned back in France. So his oldest
brother, Raymond Jr., taught him English at home. By
the time my father became fluent, though, he had fallen
two grades behind. He also had trouble getting along
with his teachers. Finally, by the time he reached the
ninth grade, he decided to drop out. Make no mistake,
though: he may have lost his desire to attend school,
but he certainly did not lose his desire to learn. My
father was a smart man, and while he worked, he continued to educate himself by whatever means possible.

Even though he was only seventeen when he discovered my mother was pregnant, Daddy was excited
about having a baby. He couldn't wait until I was born.
My mother, on the other hand, was scared about how
becoming a mother would change her life. She was an
honor student and had plans to go to college. Never-
theless, she thought that with the support of her family
she could still pursue her dreams *and* be a mom. However, things did not go as smoothly as she had hoped.

Seeing as there were already too many bills to pay
and a lot of mouths to feed, Grandma Justine's first
reaction was to advise my mother to abort the baby. She
was simply trying to ensure I wouldn't become another
poor soul born into a desperate situation. She couldn't
afford to send Momma to a doctor, but she did know of
"other ways" to take care of the problem.

Momma was confused and scared by this troubling advice, especially because it came from someone she loved and respected. She believed her mother to be a godly woman, and she trusted whatever she said. Despite her trepidation, since her mother said a self-induced abortion was the best thing to do, Momma decided to do it.

Fortunately for me, after several failed attempts, Momma resolved to go through with the pregnancy, even though it meant going against her mother's wishes. To her relief, Grandma Justine's response was, "If it didn't work, maybe that's because God didn't want it to work."

From that moment on there was no turning back. Momma's entire family chipped in to help prepare for my arrival. Grandma Justine even bought her a brand new white crib. Somehow they found a space for it among the other beds. My aunt gave my mother diaper service for a year and passed on the clothes her daughter, Donna, had outgrown. It turned out there would be room for me after all.

Even though my life had been spared long enough to allow my mother's pregnancy to go full term, my struggles weren't over yet. As a child, my mother's pelvic bone had been crushed in a car accident. This caused complications during labor because there wasn't enough room for me to pass through her misshapen pelvic bone. Things reached a point where the doctors said they could either save Momma or me but not both of us. Showing remarkable courage for a teenager, Momma offered to sacrifice her life to let me live.

Despite this selfless decision, during the cesarean operation, my head got caught in her pelvic bone. They tried everything, but it looked as though they would have to break my neck to get me out. If they didn't, both my mother and I would die. Just then, another doctor burst into the room. He believed he could save us both, without breaking my neck, and that is exactly what he did. On January 28, 1968, at 3:00 a.m., I entered the world. So for a second time, my life was spared. I never did find out the doctor's name, but I am forever grateful to him.

Shortly after I was born, Grandma Justine took one look at me and said, "I'm so glad that 'thing' you tried didn't work. This is *my* grandbaby!" The mere sight of me confirmed in her heart that the failed abortion attempts were God's doing. She and Grandpa Ben were so excited to have me in the house. Grandpa Ben even got all cleaned up just to take a picture with me. Momma said they looked at me so differently. It was as if they saw some sort of promise in me. I think Momma sensed there was something special about me as well. As soon as she found out she was pregnant, she said if I was a girl she would call me Kimberly Nadine. A couple of years ago I learned that this name I'd been given actually means, "beautiful hope."

On November 1, 1968, my parents decided to get married, much to my paternal grandmother's dismay. Grandma Esther didn't want her son to get involved with Momma because of where she lived. To put it bluntly, she didn't think Momma was good enough for her son. She never said that directly to Daddy, but she made her point loud and clear to Momma. Even though Daddy's parents didn't know our family personally, they knew the neighborhood … and my Grandpa Ben's reputation. Daddy came from a middle-class neighborhood where "colored" people owned homes. They even had yards with grass and drove their own cars. We lived in a place known as "The Bottom." Its name was fitting, seeing as it was definitely the bottom in terms of socioeconomic status. When Grandma Esther finally did come to see me, I was two weeks old. To her surprise, she found that I was clean and well kept, which did not fit her stereotype of the "ghetto" in which I lived. Still, it was many more years before she changed her opinion of Momma.

After my parents got married, Daddy, who had joined the army, was transferred to Aschaffenburg, Germany. Following my first birthday, Momma and I joined him there, where we lived for the next two years. When we arrived, however, Momma discovered that Daddy was not the same man she had married.

He and the other black soldiers were the targets of extreme racism from the white American soldiers, including upper-level officers. They were supposed to be on the same side, and yet black soldiers were being brutally beaten and killed by their own comrades. As a result, Daddy became a militant and started meeting with the Black Panthers. These soldiers numbed their pain with drugs like marijuana, hashish, and an assortment of pills.

In an effort to suppress his own anger and pain, Daddy started using drugs as well. But it didn't do any good. When he got high, he was quick-tempered and abusive. The combination of workplace stress and the drugs turned him into a completely different man. Momma, who was only nineteen years old at the time, often cried herself to sleep—but quietly, so as not to invite more of his wrath.

Despite Daddy's drug use, we did experience a few good family times in Germany. We went on long walks and visited places like Johannisburg Castle, where we saw a painting of the *Black Madonna and Child.* Incidentally, when they explained the painting to me, that was the first time I can remember hearing the name Jesus. My favorite place to be as we explored the German countryside was on Daddy's shoulders.

Momma says I had such a love for Daddy. I would cry when he left for work. And when he returned home after working a double shift, I ran down the hall in my "footie" pajamas, screaming, "Daddy!" Other times, Daddy would come home from work and show me how to do forward rolls and handstands. As a youngster he had done acrobatic routines at different school events. There was no way any of us could have known that this seemingly insignificant activity was planting seeds for my own gymnastics career.

# TWO

# MAKING DADDY HAPPY

After a couple of years in Germany, Momma got word that Grandpa Ben was dying, so she took me back to Virginia to see him while Daddy finished out the last few months of his term of service. Grandpa Ben held on long enough to see his youngest daughter and newest granddaughter, but he died two weeks after our arrival. I was only three years old when he died, but I still remember the smell of the room where he took his last breath.

After Daddy arrived from Germany, we officially moved in with Grandma Justine. By that point, she and Grandpa Ben had moved into a better home on Cary Street that had indoor plumbing. My aunt Lois and three of her children were also staying there at the time. Momma, Daddy, and I all slept in the same bed. My aunt and cousins shared another room, and Grandma had her own room.

Every now and then I would sleep with Grandma instead. I have fond memories of sleeping on the "hill," as I called it. When Grandma lay down, the bed would sink so low on her side that the other side of the worn-out mattress would rise up, creating a large mound.

Each night it was a challenge to keep from rolling down and becoming wedged between Grandma and the mattress—not to mention trying to sleep through her monstrous snoring!

Grandma Justine was a sweet lady. She would often sit on the side of her bed and read her Bible before going to sleep. Grandma was also very active in the church. She sang in the choir and served on the usher board and the missionary board. She had her moments, as we all do, but she also had an unwavering faith in God that piqued my curiosity. She went to church most Sundays, until her knees started to bother her and it became too difficult to walk the many stairs at church. When she sat down or stood up at home, she often flinched in pain and grunted, "Gracious and merciful Father." I always wondered to whom she was talking. When she couldn't go to church, members of the church came to her with communion and prayer.

If Grandma Justine wasn't reading her Bible, she was doing a crossword puzzle. She loved puzzles of all kinds. I don't remember a single Christmas without her receiving a puzzle book or a one thousand-piece jigsaw puzzle. I spent many summer nights helping her put those puzzles together or playing cards with her and my cousins. The entire time we swatted mosquitoes and rubbed ice cubes on our face and neck to keep cool as the rusty old fan circulated the hot, humid air.

On summer days I would play with my cousins in the backyard, which was mostly dirt with patches of grass here and there. That didn't bother us, though. One of our favorite activities was baking mud pies on the homemade fence that ran along the back alley. We used mud for meat, grass for greens, and smooth rocks for potatoes. I spent many happy hours covered in dirt from my freshly braided hair to my makeshift sandals that my grandma fashioned for me out of worn-out shoes that were too small.

Throughout this time, my parents' relationship was still quite rocky. Sometimes they were together, sometimes not. It broke my mother's heart to hear about Daddy being seen at concerts and parties with other women. He was out having a good time while she sat at home watching TV with me. He had been her first and only love, and she had hoped for a marriage that would bring joy. Instead, it brought only pain. The intensity of the pain increased with every act of unfaithfulness and neglect. My mother was so unhappy, and yet she always did her best to keep me happy.

When my parents finally broke up for good (or so it seemed), she worked even harder and strived for excellence in all she did. She worked as a bank teller downtown and was eventually promoted to supervisor. She often took me to work with her on Saturdays. While she earned overtime wages, I sat at a desk and pretended to be a grown-up. She loved to dream, and she refused to settle for anything less than achieving her goals. And yet, as a divorced, single mom in her early twenties, the odds were definitely against her.

Eventually, she landed a job that paid enough for us to move out of Grandma Justine's and into a small single-bedroom apartment that was attached to the rear of a beauty parlor. I remember that the kitchen had a brown linoleum floor. In the living room were a black pleather sofa and chair. Draped across the back of the sofa was a hand-crocheted red, black, and green afghan, which represented Black Power. My mother had made it herself, and she proudly displayed it for all to see. It symbolized black unity and the goal of resurrecting pride in the African-American culture. To me, "black pride" spoke of the possibility that we might succeed in life and overcome the racial barriers that had held us back for so long.

Momma took me to church every Sunday. We walked hand in hand through Maymont and Byrd Parks and into the halls of Riverview Baptist Church. I would go to Sunday-school class for first graders, and Momma was my teacher. Each week we had playtime, followed by Bible stories and songs. It was great. I didn't understand a whole lot, but I did leave knowing that God loved all the little children of the world. When church was over, we walked back home through the park, where I collected acorns. I'd take them home, put them in an ashtray, and stir them while mimicking Momma as she cooked the Sunday meal. On Sundays, we ate a larger meal than we did on the weekdays. I usually did so sitting on sheets of newspaper on the floor while watching a Shirley Temple movie. Back then, Sundays were always peaceful and happy.

Daddy would still drift in and out of our lives on occasion. He would show up one day promising to change, and my mother would take him back in, only to endure the same heartache of infidelity and drug addiction after his initial enthusiasm wore off.

Marijuana was common in our home when Daddy was around. He grew it like houseplants. Sometimes he would have parties at our place. As he and his friends smoked up, drank, or did whatever other drugs they happened to bring along, Momma and I would sit in our bedroom and watch TV. She wasn't into that scene at all. She had tried to fit in by smoking marijuana, but it just wasn't for her, and she didn't want me to become a part of it either. However, with so much of it in the house, it was only a matter of time before I got involved.

I was six or seven when Daddy first taught me how to roll joints. I became quite good at it. I could use the rolling machine or do it freestyle, using only my fingers. During one of his parties, he called me into the smoke-filled room to show off my skills. As I sat across from his friends and rolled them each a joint, it dawned on me that I was finally doing something "right" in his eyes! He was actually proud of me! That made me want to learn even more about how to handle drugs.

When I was around nine, I took things a step further by actually smoking a joint that was given to me by an adult, who was very close to me. My parents never knew about it. It was more of an experiment than a habit. Yet any habit I could have developed may have been easily satisfied while sitting in the smoke-filled rooms, as I often did, getting contact highs from inhaling the secondhand smoke.

Later, at the age of thirteen, I would continue my quest to gain more knowledge about drugs. A drug dealer had moved in next door to Grandma Justine. I knew that drugs were not something the *older* generation approved of, but I didn't realize how serious it was from a legal standpoint. Drugs were such an everyday part of life that it didn't seem out of the ordinary to be around them. My older cousin, who was now around twenty-two, had become friends with the dealer. She was telling me about this new drug that had come out and how he knew how to make it. I was fascinated because I had a desire to understand the ins and outs of drugs, and there was a certain excitement about learning something new.

When my cousin was about to go next door, I told her that I wanted to go too. I climbed across the banister that separated the porches and entered through the front door. When we went in, we found him at work making a new drug that would later become known as crack. I was mesmerized as I watched him go through the various steps to create the drug. I followed each step closely because I felt if I could learn this new skill, I would *really* make my daddy proud. Then I sat there and watched him smoke some of it from a weird-looking pipe. I inhaled the smoke as he put the bowl of the pipe beneath my nose. It created a burning sensation in my nostrils and had a strong, unpleasant odor. Even though I stayed there a while longer, I had no desire to experiment with the drug any further. That was my first and last experience with crack, though I would see its effects on others for years to come.

I thought my newfound knowledge would make Daddy proud of me one day. I had no idea if Daddy even knew about this drug yet, but if the situation ever presented itself, I wanted to be ready. Thankfully for both of us, that occasion never arose.

I would have done anything to see Daddy smile at me. There were times when I just couldn't get enough of him, like the times we sat with Momma at the kitchen table and recorded ourselves singing funny songs. I would laugh until my belly hurt and beg him to sing a little longer. Once, after he took me to the doctor downtown, instead of getting me back to school, he used our bus fare to take me to a museum instead. He had such a love for history. Had his school experience been more positive, I'm sure he would have become a history teacher. Through him, I developed a love for history too. Of course, I liked whatever Daddy liked. He took me on nature walks down by the James River. We'd see snakes and other animals, and he always knew an interesting fact about them. I thought he was the smartest man in the world.

At first, it was nice having Daddy back in the picture. He was funny and silly, and we laughed a lot. Early each morning he would wash and blow-dry his hair. When I heard the blow dryer, I knew he was almost ready to leave for work. He looked so handsome in his white uniform, and he always prided himself on being punctual. For a while we were a happy family again ... well, almost happy.

Daddy was a perfectionist, and he had very high standards for himself and others. As a result, he was always very critical. Shortly after he moved in, his complaints began to increase. Sometimes they were directed at me, but even when he was criticizing Momma, I still took them personally. I became obsessed with being perfect and making him happy so there would be no yelling or disappointment. To me, if he was happy, that meant he loved us. His anger represented love lost. Unfortunately, I began to see a lot of love lost in our home, until that fleeting sense of peace disappeared forever.

Some days, everything would be fine. He'd have a good job and go to work every day. Momma said his bosses always praised his excellent work. Then out of nowhere, Momma would get a call saying Daddy was in jail. I never knew why he was in trouble, but I remember going down to the jail with Momma to visit him. I knew it was a place where bad people went, so before we got there, I was a little afraid. When we entered the building, everything seemed to echo. The walls were white, cold, and sterile. Momma was calm. If she had any fear or hesitancy, she didn't show it. Once we were allowed to go in, I sat on Momma's lap and looked at Daddy through a thick glass window. He smiled at me and touched the glass, and I put my hand up to his. I spoke with him on the phone that connected us, and he carried on as if everything were okay. I was curious but no longer scared. However, I felt sad for Daddy, and all I wanted to know was when he was coming home.

At home, as an only child, I spent a great deal of time alone. But I always found plenty of creative ways to entertain myself. One of my favorite things to do was line up my stuffed animals on the sofa and then interview them as if I were hosting a TV show. My favorite was a purple elephant that Daddy won for me at the state fair. I usually started the show with, "Welcome to National Geographic. I'm your host, Kim Hamilton."

Then I interviewed the animals about their lives and habitats. I would even speak proper English, like they did on real television, and I would often record myself on a tape recorder that I got for Christmas. As a second grader, I had always been quite shy, but I came out of my shell, on cue, before the imaginary cameras. Sometimes as I hosted this fictitious show, I heard my parents arguing in the next room. That only made me focus all the more on the sound of my voice and the stuffed animals' imaginary replies.

Yet, I would continue to hear my mother pleading. The tears welled up in my eyes, butterflies filled my stomach, and sadness flooded my entire body. I stretched open my eyes to prevent the tears from streaming down my face. *The show must go on.* I pressed through with the interviews until I found myself sobbing as I interrogated the lifeless animals. But I would not stop the interview until *I* wanted to stop. So I continued my small talk with a raised voice to drown out the arguing and would not cease until I heard silence from the other room, which usually followed a slamming front door. *He's gone.*

Those animals became my best friends. They served as a source of sanity and strength during that tumultuous time. I needed someone with whom to share my sadness, and since I didn't have any siblings, those lifeless objects were my only substitute. I never told anyone what went on in our home. It wasn't that my parents told me to hide it. It just never occurred to me that so much conflict was abnormal. I thought everyone's home was just like mine. The only one with whom I did share my troubles was Jesus. I couldn't see him or hear him, but I heard Momma thank him every night before she went to sleep.

The few occasions when my parents didn't argue really stand out. I remember one time when we took a ride in Daddy's mid-70s model Buick Electra 225, known in my neighborhood as "a deuce and a quarter." My parents were in the front seat, and I was in the back with my favorite doll baby. It was so nice and peaceful. That scene became my definition of happiness. I wanted to have a husband one day who would drive the car while I sat in the passenger seat and our children sat in the back. That was the way things were supposed to be, I thought. To this day, when I go for a drive with my husband, Corwin, I get a happy feeling of peace. It amazes me how such a simple thing can still mean so much.

Try as I might, it was impossible for me to avoid my parents' fights in that little apartment. On one occasion I was sitting on our bed watching TV while my parents screamed at each other just outside the door. I tried to focus on the sound of the TV, but the fighting kept getting louder, and I was scared Daddy was going to get violent. Then I heard a loud bang. I leapt up, determined to help my momma, even though I was still only in elementary school.

When I opened the bedroom door, I saw Momma lying on the floor and Daddy standing over her. My eyes widened with fear, and my little heart beat so fast I could hear it pounding in my ears. I was so afraid Momma was hurt and that Daddy would hurt me next. Momma quickly told me that she was okay and that she had just fallen down. Then she told me to go back into the bedroom. Later she came in and told me that Daddy had pushed her a little but that it was just an accident. I wanted to believe her, but I couldn't understand how all that commotion could merely be the result of a mishap.

Still, another night, I heard Momma screaming and pleading with Daddy in the bathroom. When I walked in, I discovered my father trying to take his own life, while Momma struggled to stop him. They slammed against the walls, the window, and the mirror, but she would not give up the fight. No matter how he had treated her, she loved him and had not relinquished hope that things could change.

The fate of suicide had plagued Daddy's African-American army buddies. They were still scarred by what had happened to them in Germany some seven years before. They spent countless hours together trying to find healing, but in all the wrong places. Most of them would take the path of suicide as Daddy tried to do that night. Sadly, those who lived would still continue to suffer as every single one of them ended up losing their families. Daddy was fighting an uphill battle, and the odds were against him.

I stood there emotionless. The only tears I shed in that moment were for my mother, who was so distraught and sad. Daddy was also sobbing, but as I stood there watching, I wished he would just go through with it. Then we wouldn't have to be scared or sad anymore. All our problems would be over. I was eight years old.

Obviously, the emotional abuse I experienced had begun to take its toll. From then on my feelings for my father became a combination of love, fear, and anger. Every time I heard his keys jingle outside, panic washed over me because I didn't know what kind of person would walk through the door. If he were high, he would be happy. If not, look out. Even as an adult, I still feel anxious when I hear my husband's keys at the door—not that Corwin is anything like my father was, but old habits die hard.

Momma's mood changed whenever he was there too. She'd go from being playful and fun to being quiet and very careful about everything she said and did. Her goal was the same as mine: to keep the peace. I still wanted to please my daddy, but now it wasn't just a matter of making him love me. I also wanted to make sure he didn't get angry and hurt Momma or me.

My anger toward my father was present and very real, but I turned it inward for the most part, and I even took some of it out on Momma. I just couldn't understand why she continued to allow him back into our lives when he caused so much pain. But in spite of his ways, she still loved him and always held out hope that things would change for the better, someday.

# THREE

# GYMNASTICS? GIRL, PLEASE!

It was the summer of 1976, while visiting Grandma Justine, that I discovered gymnastics. I was eight years old, and my eyes were glued to the television screen as Nadia Comaneci wowed the world with her perfect performances during the Summer Olympics in Montreal. I had never seen anything more beautiful. On each event, she floated effortlessly. Her flips and spins mesmerized me as she maneuvered in ways I had never seen the human body move before. I imagined how free she must have felt as she defied gravity. With every perfect landing, I coveted her control. My brief life experiences had already left me feeling caged and powerless to affect anything around me. I wanted freedom. I wanted power. I wanted gymnastics!

"I can do that!" I said. Then I leaped up, ran across the carpet, and flipped forward onto my back. The boom created by my landing shook the entire house. Yet the feeling of flying through the air gave me a sense of euphoria. The adults, who were visiting in the kitchen, were none too happy with my little circus act.

To absorb the sound of my body crashing to the floor, I constructed a landing pad out of pillows. That worked for a while, but as I became bolder and the tricks got bigger, I was ordered to take my act outside.

A splinter-filled wooden porch capped off a set of concrete stairs that led down to the sidewalk outside Grandma Justine's house. This became my "gymnasium," where I practiced all kinds of flips. My goal was to do a side flip with no hands. Seeing as Grandma wouldn't let me take her pillows outside, I had to be smart in order to survive. I started out by standing on the first stair and flipping down onto the sidewalk. I practiced every day until I could do it with no hands. Then I taught myself how to do it on a flat surface. Years later I learned that expert coaches use this same type of progression to teach skills to their gymnasts. I continued to learn all kinds of tricks, including the side aerial, which is a no-hands cartwheel. I'd flip up and down the street, off stairs and walls, anywhere I could. Best of all, I was really good at it. I felt that I had discovered my calling.

Each day that summer we raced down to the bus stop so we could meet Grandma Justine after work. She wobbled back home with us on her arthritic knees, her bag slung over her arm. It always had just enough peppermints inside to share with everyone. She was usually tired, but she always had time to watch my latest trick. "Look, Gramma! Look what I can do!" I would say. Afterward her reply was always the same: "Girl, you gon' bust your head w-i-i-i-de open!"

Things reached a point where Momma was worried I was literally going to kill myself if I pushed myself any further, so she looked around for a place where I could train for real. It turned out that a good friend of mine, a little white girl at my school named Patricia, was taking gymnastics, and her mother gave us contact information for her gym. Momma saw potential in me, even if the idea of a poor little black girl from the wrong side of town becoming a gymnast sounded a little crazy. She was my biggest cheerleader. I had no idea how much I would come to rely on her encouragement in the days and years to come.

After a few months passed, Daddy persuaded Momma that he was finally ready to give up his relationships with other women and get on the right path for good. He had a good job as an assistant at a hospital and was ready to be a family man again. Convinced he really meant it this time, they remarried on July 2, 1977. Momma felt she was doing the right thing, and she wanted me to grow up in a two-parent household. But for me, this meant that I would now have to cope with the love, anger, and fear I had for my father on a *daily* basis.

Shortly after my parents remarried, we were forced to leave the apartment behind the beauty parlor. The owner wanted to rent it to a family member instead. Again, Grandma Justine allowed us to move back in with her. She always made us feel welcomed at her house, but I can't say the same for everyone else who lived there.

One of my cousins, who was nine years older, was maliciously cruel to me. She teased me all the time and encouraged another cousin, Donna, to do the same.

She'd even coax us into fistfights for her amusement. Her constant teasing ranged from telling me how she had seen my father with his "other" family in the park to making fun of my full lips. For this reason, I spent most of my life clenching my lips together in a vain effort to make them appear smaller. Over fifteen years later, I learned that Daddy really did have another family, which was a painful reality for me. My relatives on his side knew about his other family and helped him keep it a secret from us. Daddy's other family even knew about Momma and me, but we would be the *last* to know about them.

My cousin would also tell lies about me to see me get in trouble. She called me demeaning names and degraded me using terms so derogatory, vulgar, and foul that I've chosen not to give the words power by putting them in print. She took special pleasure in making me cry. It seemed as if she did everything in her power to make me feel ashamed, worthless, and like my life didn't matter. Listening to her made me feel as if I didn't belong in the family and that I was just a "mistake," a baby that wasn't wanted. Maybe she was privy to my grandmother's directive to abort me. Despite the way she treated me, I was so desperate to get on her good side that I did whatever she wanted me to do, even if it meant being mean and hateful to someone else by treating them with the same disdain she had treated me.

Despite her efforts to pit us against each other, my cousin Donna and I remained close. I also spent a lot of time with my other cousins, Lamont and Marlon.

Lamont was Donna's little brother. Marlon was an only child like me, so we pretended to be brother and sister. When we got together we usually played "Charlie and Barbara," a TV show we made up where the two of us were crime-solving cops. We even had a theme song that we sang at the beginning and end of each show. After we solved the latest case, we went to Max's Bar (Grandma Justine's kitchen), where we drank iced tea from a shot glass, pretending it was scotch. To us, drinking alcohol was the grown-up thing to do. Lamont and Marlon were a couple of years younger than me, but we loved being together; unlike my mean cousin, they never made fun of me.

This dynamic definitely created a pattern for my future relationships. Even throughout my high school and college years, I found it easier to relate to guys than girls. Of course, that probably also had a lot to do with me being a tomboy. I spent many happy days with my cousins, digging up worms, playing with Hot Wheels cars, catching June bugs, tying a piece of thread around one of their legs so we could fly them around like a pet on a leash, and putting lightning bugs in jelly jars so we could watch them at night.

We'd also put on plays, using a neighbor's back porch as a stage. In addition to the performance, we'd string up pictures we had drawn on the clothesline and sell them, along with red or grape Kool-Aid, which we served in tiny paper cups. Even at twenty-five cents per head, we always attracted a good crowd. People didn't mind that we had no chairs, just as long as we were putting our imaginations to good use.

Another way we earned money was by filling plastic cups with dirt and flowers that we had picked from neighbors' yards and then selling these "bouquets" door-to-door. People paid up to a quarter for them, and they didn't even seem to mind that they were buying back their own flowers.

Our block was filled with people who made us feel special. There was a lady we called Aunt Ethel (pronounced Alpha), who gave us candy. There was also Miss Arti-T, the cat lady. She must have had fifty cats in her house! Mr. Hope was better known to us as "the popsicle man" because he gave us popsicles almost every day. Then there was Mrs. Jenkins. We loved her because she gave out full-sized candy bars on Halloween! With such people in our neighborhood, we felt free to run up and down the streets without ever fearing for our safety. In retrospect, maybe there *should* have been more fear. I do remember finding and playing with used syringes in the empty lot at the corner. I'd pick up the ones that weren't too dirty and play doctor by pretending to give myself shots. No worries though, the needles were not in them. I always wondered where they came from since there were no doctors in the neighborhood or any medical facilities nearby.

Sometimes, I heard gunshots at night and every now and then during the day. There was even a little boy my age who was killed in a drive-by shooting while he played outside in broad daylight. But when we were young, our biggest fear wasn't getting shot. It was Matoo, a wild-haired lady who lived two doors down from us. Each day she sat out on her porch in the same dirty brown dress, chewing tobacco. We had to be careful whenever we ran past her place, which was often, because we were terrified of getting hit by the brown stream of slimy spit that she "h-h-hocked" every few minutes. She could spit over ten feet from her porch to the street. We knew that if we got hit we'd have to live the rest of our lives with a nickname like "Snuff-neck Skippy" or worse. Rumor had it that her spit could eat through our skin.

For entertainment on Friday nights we lay in bed and looked out the window as the people across the street drank and got into fights. We also watched people walk up and down the street and tried to guess whether they were on their way to do a drug deal or returning home from one. Sometimes we saw people who had committed serious crimes, like murder, but who had yet to be caught. We didn't have reality TV back then; we just had reality.

# FOUR

# LITTLE BLACK GIRL IN A WHITE GIRL'S WORLD

It was three months before my tenth birthday. We didn't have a car, so Momma and I had to ride the bus to my first gymnastics class, on a Saturday morning. The gym was called the Richmond Olympiad. If anyone in Virginia was serious about a career in gymnastics, he or she needed to train there. Gordon and Judy Shaw owned the gym. They were a young couple with no children of their own, but the hundreds of little gymnasts they coached more than compensated for this lack. As we entered the building, it felt so huge and intimidating. It was full of little kids running, jumping, twisting, and flipping. As I looked around, I realized I was the only little black girl there. I stood out even more in my T-shirt and shorts, which I wore because I didn't own a leotard.

Despite my initial feelings of trepidation, that first class was so much fun. Everything they told me to do was easy. Walking and jumping on the balance beam was a snap. I had already been doing that on concrete walls, some of them fifteen feet high. Bounding across the makeshift vaulting horse was not a challenge either.

I'd vaulted over higher obstacles like chain link fences, stair rails, porches, and even people. So when I was surrounded by soft cushy mats in gymnastics class, I flipped around like a mad woman, not worrying about getting hurt at all. At one point I wanted to try more difficult skills, so I climbed onto the uneven bars and started swinging around. I made my way to the very top of the high bar without any struggle at all. I was enjoying myself until the instructors reprimanded me.

After class the coaches called me over. I thought they were going to scold me again for my exploits on the uneven bars. Instead, they asked if I had taken gymnastics lessons before. When I explained how I had taught myself on the brick sidewalk in front of my house, the coaches asked what else I could do. So I showed them my side aerials, cartwheels, and walkovers. They were impressed enough to ask me if I wanted to join their gymnastics team and start competing. I didn't hesitate for a second. "Yes!" My mother also agreed, though neither of us really had any idea of what we were about to get into.

I needed a leotard, so they took me into their pro shop. I picked out a green V-neck leotard with a zipper up the front. I thought it was the most beautiful thing in the world. I chose green because I knew it was Daddy's favorite color. I was still trying to gain his approval. Momma couldn't afford the leotard, so my coaches told her she could just pay for it when she got the money. I am so grateful for the generosity they showed to Momma and me that day. They were about to open the door to a world I never knew existed, an act of kindness that would change the course of my life. Best of all, they did not discriminate against me because of my color. My skill was all that mattered.

From that point on, I started training with the team. The team consisted of three levels: Class I, II, and III. I started off with the Class IIIs, which were the beginners, and we trained three days a week. At first, it was difficult for Momma to get me to practice because she didn't have a car and couldn't get away from work to ride with me on the bus. But it turned out that Patricia (who told me about the gym) was also on the team, so Momma arranged for me to carpool with her.

It took most students a full year to prepare for competition, but it only took me eight weeks. When I was ten years old, I qualified for the Class III Virginia state meet. I was moving up in the world. I had added a black leotard to my wardrobe, so I now had two choices for practice, and at the state meet I wore our official competition uniform, which was white with long sleeves. It was also a special treat to wear the red team sweat suit with *Olympiad* across the back. I felt like an Olympian. Momma, Daddy, his older brother, and his girlfriend all drove down to Hampton, Virginia, to watch me compete.

Something else special happened during that meet that made a lasting impression on me: I saw another little black gymnast, which was extremely rare in those days. I remember watching her do a beautiful arched dive roll, which was part of the compulsory routine. Somehow I had gotten it into my head that I could never measure up to the little white girls, so I didn't even try. But as I watched her perform the skill so well, it gave me permission to strive for the same level of excellence. That was a pivotal moment in my fledgling career. No longer would I settle for just getting by and believing that the little white girls would always be better. All that mattered was achieving perfection. Largely, as a result of my attitude change that day, I won third place on floor exercise. Not bad for my very first state competition.

Over the next couple of years, I excelled and moved up through the ranks. When I was eleven years old, I was invited, along with select members of the Richmond Olympiad Class II team, to my first international competition. Momma and Daddy were there to see me off. For the first time since I was a toddler, I flew on a plane, all the way to Bermuda. I was nervous and excited at the same time. I was nervous about being away from my family but excited to experience a new country with my coach and my teammates.

Each family was required to pay their own daughter's way. However, we could not afford to do so and had to rely upon donors to cover *my* expenses. Momma was a little uneasy about me going so far without her, but Daddy kept telling her I would be all right. They both knew it was an opportunity of a lifetime. Back then, it wasn't common to see black Americans traveling internationally, especially from my neighborhood.

Bermuda was so different from my life on Cary Street. I swam in beautiful blue waters with pink sand beaches. Nobody at home would believe that. During the competition we stayed with a host family who had a beautiful home in the hills. I shared a bedroom with their oldest daughter, Linda, who was also a gymnast.

Having no siblings of my own, I was fascinated by the way Linda interacted with her younger sister and brother. It was so unlike my situation at home.

Although this was my first international competition, I won first place on four events. We were required to do both compulsory and optional routines. The compulsories were standard routines, which required each gymnast to perform the same skills. Optional routines allowed us to showcase our personalities and mastery of individual skills. I won the compulsory vault and uneven bars and optional bars and floor exercise. That surprised everyone, especially me. That trip also had a huge impact on me mentally. For perhaps the first time, my perspective was broadened beyond the confines of my neighborhood. I went on to have a successful season as a Class II gymnast and it culminated with the All-Around win at the Class II Virginia State meet. As I competed internationally, my view of the world continued to expand, until it became impossible for me to be satisfied with anything local. I wanted everything I did and every influence I had to occur on a statewide, national, and international level.

During the summer I trained from nine in the morning until one in the afternoon. It took forty-five minutes to ride the bus across town, so I had to get up early. My cousin (the one who teased me so much when I was younger) would ride with me to the gym. She was a lot nicer to me now for some reason. We had to transfer downtown and then take another bus across the river, which would let us off a half mile from the gym. Then we walked to the gym by way of an industrial park. Sometimes we'd stop at a grocery store and buy donuts. My cousin sat and watched while I worked out. When practice was over I rushed to put my clothes on over my leotard. Then, with white chalk all over me from the uneven bars, we would run for the bus, pay our fare, get the transfer, then finally sit down and relax for the trip home.

During this time I really wanted to learn one gymnastics skill in particular, a round-off back handspring with a full twisting layout. If I could pull it off, I would have a better chance of moving up to the next competitive level. I worked at it time and time again during practice, but it still wasn't clicking.

I wanted Daddy to help me master the full twisting layout, so I explained to him how the coaches spotted me at the gym. He picked up additional tips on his own, by watching the coaches, and quickly became confident that he could assist me. Sometimes he would take me to the playground or to Maymont Park so he could help me work on this difficult skill. Once we found a grassy, level spot, Daddy would take his place a few yards away from me. Then I would run three steps and do a round-off back handspring right into his arms. He caught me and then helped me to mimic a full twisting layout as he held me in the air. I did this repeatedly until he felt I was ready to try the entire skill. "Don't drop me, Daddy!" I yelled to him. "I won't!" he said before making a silly face, as if he was afraid he might. My life was literally in his hands at that point because there was no mat to break my fall, only the grass.

The first time I tried the full skill, my arm bopped him in the head. He caught me in midair anyway, but I was too scared to try it again. Daddy persisted, though, taking me back to the first step again and then working me through each step. With his help I was finally able to pull it off. Of course, by this point we had attracted quite a crowd, which served to make my achievement even sweeter. With determination and hard work, I finally mastered the full twisting layout. It wasn't easy learning this skill, but I felt a tremendous sense of accomplishment, seeing how my perseverance paid off.

In the fall of 1979, I graduated from Class II Intermediate to Class I Advanced. My new coach would be James (Jim) Roe. One of my first meets as a Class I was in Nova Scotia, Canada, where I won silver medals on vault, bars, and beam, and gold medals on floor and in the all-around. That year, I achieved more than I expected, ending the season with a second place finish in the all-around at the Class I state meet.

As I progressed through the ranks, my coaches wanted me to train every day. Because my cousin couldn't spend all of her time taking me to and from practice, my parents saved up enough money for a deposit on an apartment located right behind the gym. I was so happy because now I could practice as much as I wanted without worrying about how I was going to get there.

I was twelve years old and heading into the seventh grade when we made the big move. Our relocation from the West End to Southside, however, meant that Momma had to commute to her job by bus, which took one and a half hours each way. It was a huge sacrifice. She could have easily refused, bringing my gymnastics career to a sudden halt. But she always put me first. She knew her little girl had to get to the gym, and she was willing to sacrifice anything to make it happen. She was always doing things like that. If we had only three pieces of meat for dinner and my daddy wanted two, she would give up her piece. If I were still hungry after I'd finished my plate of food, she would give me the rest of hers and go without. Neither my daddy nor I realized what she was doing. She always made it seem as if she wasn't hungry and insisted we take it.

Momma would also go without clothing, wearing the same two or three dresses and the same shoes every day. I remember her shoes being so worn out that the sole had pulled away from the bottom of one shoe and I could see inside the heel. For years she made all of my clothing. When I got to the age where I wanted store-bought clothes like my classmates, she and Daddy sacrificed even further, scraping up enough money to buy me a different outfit for each day of the week. Lack of finances and discouragement from her parents had killed Momma's dream of becoming a professional dancer when she was young, so she was determined not to allow the same thing to happen to me.

Even though I had an outfit for each day of the week, one school night I found out that I needed to wear a skirt the following day for a special event. The problem was that all of my outfits were pants. My daddy came to the rescue by offering to walk two miles to the mall with me so I could buy a skirt. It was 8:00 p.m. when we left, and the stores closed at nine. If we hurried, we just might make it. We walked quickly in the dark, cutting across parking lots and jumping across ditches. Then we walked down the turnpike toward the endless stream of oncoming headlights. The most harrowing part was crossing the exit and entry ramps without getting hit. Despite the danger, I was more afraid that one of my school friends would drive past and see me. If someone saw me, the word would have quickly spread among my peers. This would have been a devastating blow to a soft-spoken outsider like me, who was desperately trying to fit in. I held my head down the entire time, glancing up only occasionally to see how much farther we had to go.

By the time we reached the mall, we had only fifteen minutes before the stores closed. I had envisioned getting a stylish outfit that would make me look sophisticated, something worthy of a magazine cover. I was certain that once I wore that skirt, the boys who didn't pay attention to me would be struck by my womanly beauty. But as we rifled through the racks, my vision quickly faded. I found plenty of nice skirts but none my size. With time running out, I had no choice but to choose something from the little girls' section. It was an ugly pink and purple plaid skirt, but I didn't dare leave empty-handed after my daddy had walked two miles to get me there. To top things off, when we went to pay for the skirt, it cost far more than we had anticipated. But we were out of time and couldn't look for anything else. So we bought the skirt and made another trek up the turnpike and back home.

Daddy happened to be home that night to help me, and I was very grateful, but my parents' relationship was continuing to weaken. He had begun staying out all hours of the night, and he wasn't always able to contribute to the family, financially. Sometimes he was just out of work. From some of their heated discussions, I gathered that other times he just spent his money elsewhere.

Our move to Southside also meant I had to attend a new school. When Daddy found out which school I was going to attend, he felt it necessary to teach me how to defend myself. The first thing he taught me was how to take a gun out of a person's hand while he or she was pointing it at me. He had me practice the maneuver again and again until I got it right. Next, he taught me how to fight. He didn't just show me how to stun an opponent, though; he taught me how to take the opponent out for good. He taught me a couple of methods of physically engaging someone in a way that could cause death. Daddy wasn't trying to encourage me to kill anybody, but if I found myself in a life or death situation, he wanted me to be ready. I practiced the moves a lot when I was alone, especially when I was angry about the escalating tension between my parents. My imagination would get the best of me as I pictured myself taking out an enemy with speed and precision. I know now that this was Daddy's way of showing how much he loved me. He wanted to make sure I was safe. But his actions and sudden disappearances still left me feeling unloved and abandoned. I was a maze of emotions. There was a constant shift of feelings that would occur on a moment's notice. Love. Anger. Fear. Then the random cycle continued. Stability and security were absent when I needed them the most.

With all of the anger and bitterness I was harboring inside, I also developed a secret appetite for violence. With the skills Daddy taught me and the strength and power I had gained through my gymnastics training, I was afraid that if I ever did get into a fight with someone, I could literally take his or her life. So I did my best to avoid situations that would give rise to any physical confrontation.

It was my second year as a Class I, and my practices were intense now, not nearly as fun as they used to be. I still loved the power involved and the feeling of flying through the air with complete control, but the pressure was increasing, and my coach, Jim, needed me to be tough. When the skin on my hands ripped off during a bar routine, I got no sympathy from him. Jim merely pushed his finger into the open wound and laughed. Then he made me tape it up and get right back up there. My ankles and knees also began to hurt constantly. Jim trained me to work through the pain, though. After practice I shoved my feet into buckets of ice water, wrapped bags of ice around my knees, and tended to my bloodied hands. When I went to sleep at night, I put gobs of zinc oxide ointment on my hands and covered them with socks so it wouldn't get all over the sheets. My coaches told me the key to excelling in gymnastics was learning how to block out the pain while concentrating on each skill. So that's exactly what I attempted to do.

By the time I was thirteen, though, my efforts to suppress both physical and emotional pain started to catch up with me. I began to cry uncontrollably for no apparent reason. My teachers asked me what was wrong, but I couldn't tell them because I didn't know. As I reflect back on my fragile emotional state, I realize that the intensity of practice coupled with the issues at home were taking a terrible mental and physical toll. I never told a soul what was going on at home, so the sudden onslaught of uncontrollable weeping became my only emotional outlet. When I regained composure, I would suck it up, get through the rest of the school day, and then go to practice and duke it out again. But when I got back home at night, I faced the same tensions all over again.

Throughout this time, my father continued to come and go as he pleased. Sometimes he disappeared for weeks on end, which was very difficult for me. I'd get accustomed to things being a certain way without him, and then he would return home and turn my world upside down. When he wasn't there, I felt at ease. But as soon as I heard his keys jingle at the front door, I panicked and ran off to my room. As I lay there in bed, I would call upon Jesus to help us. I wanted him to be real so badly that I asked for a Bible one Christmas just so I could get to know him better. Perusing my new Bible didn't change my situation, but I must admit that there were times when I found comfort when I read it.

My father caused so much pain for my mother. Often, I heard her crying through her closed door at night. I could tell she was trying to muffle the sound by burying her face in a pillow or blanket. Every time I called out to ask what was wrong, she always said that everything was fine. But I knew it wasn't. Remarkably, throughout those years of pain, I don't remember her saying a single negative thing about my father.

During this time, Daddy's father, Grandpa Raymond, became a big part of our lives. My mother confided in Grandpa Raymond about what had been going on in our home. As a result, he filled in as a father for me when Daddy wasn't around. He also helped us out financially so we could keep the lights on, pay the rent, and continue my gymnastics training. Momma would open up and share a few of her personal struggles with Grandma Justine and with one or two other family members, but other than that, no one else knew what her life was really like.

When Daddy wouldn't come home, I felt that I wasn't worth his time. As a teenager, I struggled to figure out why I was now so unlovable. What had I done to make him abandon me? When he was home, I received praise for my gymnastics but no affirmation for who I was as a person. I don't ever remember him telling me I was pretty or smart or loved, the things little girls long to hear from their fathers. But I do remember him regularly referring to me as "boy," which I figured he did because he wished that I were a male instead of a female. And I remember him calling me "Bucky Beaver" because of the gap between my two front teeth. The combination of his sporadic absences, which grew more frequent as time passed, the ridicule of his words, and his rough treatment cut me very deeply. I was at an age where I was trying to discover who I was, and when I looked to him for answers, I found that I was *nothing*. So I had to keep my game face on all the time to avoid more pain and humiliation from those around me. I was also afraid to have too much fun because in my life, any joy I experienced was soon followed by pain. I didn't know how to articulate what I was feeling, but I figured my cousin must have been right about me being a mistake after all. My mother had no idea how much I was suffering emotionally. For years I had watched her try to hide her pain and pretend everything was okay. Now I was doing the same.

# FIVE

# GOTTA DANCE!

By the time I was thirteen, I spent so much time at the gym that my skill level increased dramatically. My ability to master certain skills so rapidly even surprised my coaches. One of my coaches, Monica, was a beautiful black woman. When I first saw her, my eyes lit up because I had never seen a black gymnastics coach before. I thought that because our skin was the same color she would be nice to me. Instead she was harder on me than on anyone else. During practice we cycled through several stations, each one focusing on a different skill that we needed to learn for our floor exercise routines. I dreaded going to Monica's station because she was especially tough on me.

One day we were working on our tour jetés, a type of leap where you kick one leg forward, do a half turn in the air while switching your legs in a scissor-like motion, and then land on the leg with which you kicked. When it was my turn I did exactly what the girls before me had done. But that wasn't good enough for Monica. She made me do it again and again. I couldn't understand why she let the others get by but was so hard on me. I concluded she didn't like me and just wanted to make my life miserable.

Later, of course, I realized that wasn't the case at all. She knew I was not an average gymnast, so she wouldn't let me get away with an average performance. She rode me time after time, enduring my pouts and dirty looks until my tour jeté resembled that of a professional ballerina. I didn't just turn and switch my legs in the air like the others. I executed a full 180-degree split in the air before I landed. Even I was amazed at my progress. I began to realize that perhaps Monica knew something I didn't.

While I was progressing quickly in all areas, Monica said the thing that would take me to the next level would be my ability to exhibit grace as well as power. To acquire that grace, she suggested I study dance. But considering that my family could barely afford my gymnastics training, never mind dance classes, we had to come up with an innovative plan to include dance in my training regimen.

It turned out Monica was friends with a local dancer named Jamie Patterson, who had moved to New York City to perform on Broadway. At that time, he was with a touring version of Bob Fosse's *All That Jazz*. When the tour stopped in Richmond, Monica invited me to come watch him perform. I was so excited. It was my first Broadway show, and I had no idea what to expect.

As we walked down the darkened aisle to our seats, which were only a few rows back from the stage, the lights came up. I was so fascinated I could barely tear my eyes away to find my seat. Then the music started, and I realized the lights had a choreography all their own. The cast sang perfectly and danced with such precision. I had never seen anything like it! As they moved across the stage, I remember asking Monica, "Which one is Jamie?"

"There he is, right over there," she replied. A moment later he was airborne in a straddle leap that was higher than I thought any human could jump. It took my breath away. I even rose slightly out of my seat. He seemed to stay up there for days! When he finally landed, he did so without a sound. He was in complete control of his body. My eyes were glued to him for the rest of the show. Here was someone from my hometown who was now living his dream in New York. That was when I first began to believe that maybe, just maybe, I could do something great with my life as well.

When Monica told Jamie about me, he offered to pay for my dance lessons. So I registered in a dance school downtown. My ballet teacher's name was Myra. Royalty was written all over her. She was tall and thin with a long neck and short dark hair. She always walked around with her back straight and her toes pointed outward in first position, while her little ballerina skirt swished back and forth across her hips with each step. I tried to imitate her perfect walk, but I don't think I ever mastered it. My jazz instructor's name was Pam. She was hip and spunky, and boy could she move! I couldn't figure out whether I wanted to be a classical ballerina or a funky jazz dancer, so I tried to be a blend of both. Because of my gymnastics schedule, I had to jump into adult evening classes, and I was the youngest dancer there. The older women stared at my long, lanky, and extremely flexible limbs with disbelief. As we worked the bar, my leg was usually lifted the highest; when we did leaps, I would float through the air. My pirouettes were quick and controlled. I was able to catch on to some elements so quickly that my instructors would modify my assignment. While others did single pirouettes, I did triples. Even though I advanced quickly, Myra and Pam always kept me challenged, and I loved every minute of it.

Myra and Pam were so excited about how I was progressing that they asked me to consider quitting gymnastics to become a dancer. I had to take some time to think about it because I really loved dance and would have loved to follow in Jamie's footsteps. In the end, though, I chose to stick with gymnastics. I couldn't shake that feeling of freedom and control I felt while flying fifteen feet in the air. I was hooked. To their credit, my parents let me make my own decision. Daddy was happy when I told him I wanted to continue with gymnastics. He had never seen any high-level black gymnasts before, and he believed that if I stuck with it, I would become a role model who could pave the way for other girls like me.

The dance classes definitely produced the desired effect. Through dance, I learned that presentation was everything. I was determined to become not only a powerful athlete but also a performer. Each routine I performed told a story. The gymnastics apparatus became my Broadway stage, and I was the star. From the moment I stepped onto the floor, I wouldn't break character until my routine was over. I fell in love with performing. It fueled my passion to be the best. I'd always been one to think outside of the box, so this was a perfect fit.

Incidentally, throughout the next several years, I didn't get to see Jamie very often. During college I ran into several different people who knew him, and I always made sure to tell them that *he* was the one who paid for my dance lessons, making it possible for me to excel as a gymnast. I got a chance to thank Jamie personally after I graduated from college.

I had moved to New York in 1992, where I performed with a company called AntiGravity. It was a unique group created by former gymnast and Broadway performer Chris Harrison. I performed with them at Carnegie Hall and in the Radio City Easter Show. While at Radio City I was approached by the manager of the Rockettes, who invited me to join the exclusive ensemble. I didn't get the chance to become a Rockette, though, because a few weeks after the invitation, my husband was traded from the New York Jets to the Green Bay Packers. But before we moved away, I worked as a dancer for a Reebok Corporate show. I was heading to the dressing room one day after rehearsing, when I heard this incredible singing echo through the hall. Captivated, I stopped to listen. After it ended, a door opened, and out walked Jamie Patterson. It turns out he had been auditioning for a part. It was so wild. There I was dancing in a show, and he was the one who had paid for my dance lessons nearly ten years earlier.

I've thanked Jamie several times since for the pivotal role he played in my career, but I don't think he can ever understand how truly grateful I am. I only hope that I can inspire and support others the same way he inspired and supported me.

# SIX

# FUNDING THE DREAM

With dance lessons covered, my gymnastics routines were getting better than ever. My dance training helped me execute my compulsory routines almost to perfection. I had fewer deductions, greater balance, and more body control. My tumbling was some of the best in the state. The newspapers followed my progress, announcing to the world when I became the first gymnast in the state of Virginia to compete a double backflip, a skill I mastered before the onset of spring floors. I ended up winning the Class I all-around gold medal in three consecutive state meets. In 1982, I was sixth in the nation in the all-around and became the first Virginian to win a national title on the uneven bars. The following year at age fifteen, I struck gold again, nearly sweeping the Region 7 Junior Olympic Championships. I earned the gold on vault, bars, floor, and the all-around, and gained a silver medal on the balance beam. In April of 1983, I competed in Junior Olympic National Championships, held at the Olympic Training Center in Colorado. I won gold medals on vault and floor and was the first African-American to become the Junior Olympic National All-Around Champion.

My teammates were my closest friends during this period. We spent many hours together in the gym, so they were the only ones in my life who understood all the hard work it took to compete in the sport. In a sense, we grew up as one and counseled each other through those tough practices. My time with them taught me so much about caring for others. As an only child, I only had to worry about me. Now I had a group of sisters who not only understood me and cared about me as a teammate, but they also cared about me as a friend. We cheered for each other, prayed for each other, and even got into trouble together. Despite our camaraderie, I never told them about my home life. I thought girls from families like theirs could never understand a family like mine. So even though we were close, I often felt alone.

Having accomplished the highest achievement a Class I gymnast could attain, as J. O. National Champion it was time to move to the next level. The pinnacle of gymnastics is the elite level. It is the level from which the Olympic teams are chosen. Only a select few would ever wear the title of "elite gymnast." In order to gain this distinction and the respect that came along with it, we had to compete in an elite qualifying meet. We were required to perform compulsory and optional routines on each event. The scores from all eight routines were combined for a total all-around score. For some, it would take multiple attempts before they scored well enough to qualify for this level. When I competed in this meet for the first time, I entered with little pressure. If I didn't do well, I would still have a chance to try again at a later date. It turned out that I would not need a second chance to qualify; the first time was a success.

The increased training and travel around the country put a tremendous strain on our family's finances. In addition to my gym fees, we had to come up with money for airfares, hotels, uniforms, meet fees, food, and so on. At first, I was able to split some of the expenses with my teammates. But when I became an elite gymnast, I had to travel alone with my coach, so the expense was all mine.

As a result, I approached my rise in the world of gymnastics with mixed emotions. I was happy with my progress, but the extra financial burden it placed on our family only added to the stress I was already experiencing. Things reached a point where I would come home from school at the end of each month and find an eviction notice on the front door because we were behind on our rent payments. It became so embarrassing that I would rush home from the school bus on those days and pull the notice off the door before any of my schoolmates could see it. When I asked my mother about the notices, she kept assuring me everything was fine. She did everything she could to prevent me from learning just how desperate she really was.

When we couldn't come up with enough money to cover my gymnastics expenses, we had to find creative ways to raise funds. Our team held yearly fund-raisers, such as selling grapefruits and oranges during the holidays or doing "cartwheel-a-thons." These methods raised some money, but it was never quite enough.

To help out, my godfather, Charlie Boy, who ran a corner store in "the Bottom," allowed us to put a can on his counter with my picture on it so his customers could donate their spare change to support my training. Eventually, he figured out he needed to bolt the can to the counter so no one would steal it. The patrons didn't have much extra income, but they pitched in whatever they could. It was a real community effort.

Seeing as so many people took an interest in helping me out, Charlie Boy thought it would be a good idea for me to spend a bit of time working in the store; that way people could see me and make a personal connection to where their money was going. However, my mother knew that groceries weren't the only things Charlie Boy sold in his store. Drugs were also sold, and Momma didn't want me to be a part of that scene. She caught a lot of flack for refusing Charlie Boy's offer. People accused her of being "uppity," saying she thought her daughter was too good to be around the people in the neighborhood. But Momma stood her ground. She didn't care what they thought or how they slandered her reputation. She was determined to do what was best for me. At the same time, she really did appreciate all that the community was doing, so she and Daddy took me down to the store often to thank those who supported me.

The owners of the gym, Gordon and Judy Shaw, were a great help when it came to figuring out innovative ways for me to raise money. Along with my coach, Monica, they hooked me up with the Corvette Club, which was a group of African-American Corvette owners who made wonderful contributions to the community. I don't know how they did it, but somehow the Shaws got the Corvette Club to donate money to offset my traveling expenses. In addition to the Corvette Club, they convinced another anonymous donor to do the same. These people didn't know me, but they believed in the hope that gymnastics had brought to my life. Somehow I was given favor with people of means, and I was able to experience far more than my circumstances would ever allow. There seemed to be a clear plan for me, and no financial barrier was going to stand in the way.

Probably the most unconventional way for us to raise money was at a nightclub called the Ebony Island. Through a connection with the Corvette Club, my parents got permission to set up a hat and coat check one Friday night. We taped handwritten numbers on wire hangers we got from the dry cleaners and then lugged them down to the nightclub to set up shop. I was well under the age limit and had never even been to a nightclub before. I tried to peek out of our station every chance I got to see what was going on inside. But it was always too dark and smoky for me to see much.

Around 1:00 a.m., they cleared the wooden dance floor and brought up the lights. Now it was time for the patrons to see where their coat check money was going. As the crowd formed a circle, I stood off to the side sheepishly in my leotard. I was really afraid of disappointing these grown-ups.

When it came time for me to take the floor, however, my sheepish stance turned into a confident strut as I put on my game face. I held my head high, swung my arms up until they were parallel to the ground, and pointed my toes with every step, exactly as I had been trained to do. Then I took my place under the rotating disco ball and began to perform. There was not enough room for me to do anything spectacular, so I had to be creative. To my surprise, the crowd was impressed and applauded my skills. Part of me was happy because this probably meant that they wouldn't ask for their money back. The other part of me thought, *If only they could see* everything *I can do. Perhaps they would be even more generous!*

By the time the nightclub closed and we had given back the last coat and hat, we had earned nearly five hundred dollars! Elated, we packed up our hangers and started our journey home. We didn't have a car, and the buses weren't running at that hour, so we had to walk the ten miles home. As I trudged along behind my parents in the wee hours of the morning, with only a thin jacket to keep out the chill, I was certain that all of my teammates were asleep in their warm beds. To keep up our spirits, we sang the "Negro National Anthem" in three-part harmony:

> *Lift every voice and sing*
> *Till earth and heaven ring,*
> *Ring with the harmonies of liberty;*
> *Let our rejoicing rise*
> *High as the listening skies,*
> *Let it resound loud as the rolling sea.*
> *Sing a song full of the faith that the dark past has taught us,*
> *Sing a song full of the hope that the present has brought us,*
> *Facing the rising sun of our new day begun*
> *Let us march on till victory is won.*

James Weldon Johnson (1871–1938)

The song reminded me that there was hope for a better day for our people. I couldn't give up. I just had to keep marching "until victory was won." Singing also took our minds off our aching feet and tired bodies. Although I was exhausted and so sore that I cried much of the way home, this was a special moment for our family. Sure, we were walking because we were too poor to afford a car. Yes, it was cold. And yes, we were exhausted. But the three of us were doing something together as a family, and that trumped all.

Despite the generosity of the nightclub patrons, the Corvette Club, and my other supporters, I still needed more money. So the Shaws allowed us to work off some of my training fees by cleaning the gym after practice. Around ten or eleven at night, after everyone else went home, we got to work. The gym was nearly twenty thousand square feet, so it was a huge job. We swept up the dust and chalk, vacuumed the carpets, cleaned the bathrooms, and put the mats and chairs in place. If we were too tired to do it at night, we woke up early and did it the following morning.

At first, Daddy did most of the work. But then he began "forgetting" to come home. When he didn't show up, Momma would get up around 5:00 a.m. to clean the gym before going off to her regular job. After working at that job for eight hours, she proceeded to her part-time job, where she worked for another four or five hours before finally coming home. I felt so badly for her. I would help out as often as I could, but after training for six hours straight, it was difficult to spend a couple of hours cleaning and then still get up for school in the morning, only to repeat the same cycle again the next day. Around the time I turned thirteen, I began to suffer from insomnia. It often prevented me from falling asleep until three or four o'clock in the morning. In spite of all this, I still managed to get A's on my report cards and repeatedly earned a spot in the National Honor Society.

Sometimes when Momma arrived at the gym early in the morning, she discovered that Daddy had slipped away from his "other life" long enough to help out. But he still didn't bother coming home to his family. Instead, when he was finished, he went right back out without even greeting her. This was his way of showing how much he cared about me, but the way he treated Momma made it difficult for me to appreciate his efforts.

My workouts were grueling and stretched later into the night. When I wasn't performing as expected, Judy Shaw's sweet face would morph into a vicious mask that would frighten a grown man. I never knew such a small woman could manifest such earsplitting rage.

"Kim Hamilton," she would yell, "you will never hold a candle to Tami Elliot!" (Tami was the only other elite gymnast who had come out of the Richmond Olympiad.) Other times, she used the names of other great athletes or my current competition, saying I would never be as good as they were. These comments tore every ounce of pride away from me as tears of embarrassment welled in my eyes. During these moments, silence came over the gym, as every single eye was on me. I felt so humiliated and ashamed. I knew Mrs. Shaw's outbursts were meant to extract a better performance, but they began to have the opposite effect instead. If you hear something negative like that enough times, eventually you start to believe it. "Why even try?" I'd ask myself sometimes. But there was something in me that wouldn't give up. I felt compelled to move forward and embrace my destiny, no matter what my circumstances were.

To close out each practice, we had to do fifteen no-fall beam routines. If we fell, we still had to finish the entire routine, but it wouldn't count toward our total. To get through it I used to play a little game in my head, where I pretended I was performing for someone I really admired. At the time I was a huge fan of Magic Johnson and the LA Lakers. So I pretended that Magic had just walked in and that I was doing my routine just for him. That thought was enough to get me through the rest of the night. My coaches had no idea what I was thinking, but it worked.

Jim and I had a love/hate relationship. Actually, hate is much too harsh. It was more like a strong dislike, but only on the bad days. Most of the time he was fun, and I knew that he cared about me a lot. But in his efforts to toughen me up, he often came across as cold and heartless. On the bad days, the very sight of him, the sound of his voice speaking my name, and the touch of his hand on my shoulder made me cringe.

Jim gave me the nickname Kemo Sabe, which is the greeting Tonto used whenever he met the Lone Ranger. According to Tonto, it meant "trusted scout." As a joke, sometimes Jim would alter the name slightly to Kemo Soggy because I was frequently in tears as I trained or competed. Either way, I thought the nickname was cool.

When I had competitions up and down the east coast, Jim would usually drive me there in his car. He had a Porsche 911, so we usually made good time. As we drove, we'd listen to his favorite music. Over time, I learned entire Supertramp, Fleetwood Mac, and John Denver albums by heart. Jim was always pleasant and caring during those rides. But when it came time for competition, I became so focused that any pleasantries he may have extended went unrecognized. Unfortunately, my focus wasn't based on confidence but on fear, especially fear of disappointing Jim. Here I was again, trying to earn a father figure's approval.

Normally, parents were not allowed to watch practices, only meets. But seeing as most of my meets were in another part of the country or another part of the world, Momma rarely got to watch me compete. On some nights, though, she was allowed to get a head start on her cleaning during my final hour of practice, which I spent alone with Jim after everyone else went home. Those times were her only chance to see my progress. Every once in a while I glanced over at her as she mopped the floors, head bowed, and caught her peeking up at me. She enjoyed every minute of it.

As if the hours I was putting in were not enough, Jim asked me to come in on Sundays to work on extra skills. Some of the elements on the compulsory uneven bar routine required me to hit a forty-five-degree angle, but he wanted me to hit ninety degrees, going straight to a handstand instead. He felt that if I pushed every element to the limit, I could outperform everyone else. Instead of Jim coming in to help me, he taught Daddy how to coach and spot me. That way, we could go into the gym any time on Sunday, using the same key we used to access the gym for cleaning.

Daddy was a good coach. I liked working with him because he was very encouraging. He followed Jim's directions and helped me perform the best uneven bar routine out there. Not only did I hit complete handstands instead of forty-five degrees on every skill possible, but as directed by Jim, I also flared my arm in a circle as I did a half pirouette on the high bar. This would later become a signature move for me. Without Jim's push to exceed expectations and the extra time Daddy put in on those Sundays, my routines would have been ordinary. With their help, I wowed the judges and raised the bar for everyone else.

Gymnastics was on my mind just about every waking minute. While lying in bed at night I'd rehearse my routines over and over again or worry about what I would have to do in practice the next day. My tomorrows were always filled with dread. Whenever my thoughts threatened to overwhelm me, I'd switch my train of thought to a fantasy life with no worries of practice, injuries, or pressure. Those fantasies provided me with the feeling of happiness I'd long for each day.

The enormity of what my mother, father, and everyone else were sacrificing to sustain my career hit home one day during practice when I was a teenager. I was angry with Jim because I felt he was being mean to me. My behavior got so out of line that he kicked me out of the gym. Thinking I was "all that," I shot back, "My mom doesn't pay for me to come here and do nothing, you know!" His reply was just as quick: "Your mom doesn't *pay* for you to come here period!" His words stung deeper than you can imagine. I had nothing to say in reply. Only later did I discover that whenever the Shaws sent my mother a bill for my training, they told her to pay what she could, when she could. A lot of the time she wasn't able to pay anything at all, but they still allowed me to train. They saw how this sport would eventually change my future and give me opportunities that wouldn't have been possible otherwise. Needless to say, I didn't speak back to Jim again—at least not where he could hear me.

The realization that our financial situation was even worse than I thought humbled me greatly. But evidently, there was still more humbling to come. One Christmas morning I woke up early, excited to see what was waiting for me under the tree. I went downstairs to the living room, where I found Momma sitting next to the tree, under which were several beautifully wrapped gifts. This was going to be a great Christmas!

"Where's Daddy?" I asked.

"I don't know. He's not here," she replied softly. I couldn't believe it. He was going to miss another holiday with us. When Daddy first started failing to show up for Thanksgiving or Christmas, Momma made up stories to cover for him when we went "house hopping" to visit other family members. She would tell them he had to work or that he wasn't feeling well. Finally, she reached the point where she got tired of covering for him, so when they asked, she'd simply say, "I don't know."

That morning, the look on her face said it all. Momma cried nearly every Christmas, and this year was no different. Whether it was because Daddy wasn't there to celebrate with us or because she couldn't afford to give me more gifts, the holidays always made her sad. She had a knack for making a little look like a lot, though. One year she got me a Polaroid One-Step camera. She wrapped the camera in one box, the flashes in another, and the batteries in another. Then she had me open the batteries first to build anticipation, followed by the flashes, and finally the camera.

I put my arms around Momma and sat there in silence while her body shook with sobs. All I could think of was why Daddy didn't love me enough to come home for Christmas. Did I do something wrong? I thought back to the last time I saw him. Did I do something to upset him? I couldn't think of anything. Not wanting to add to Momma's disappointment, I "manned up" and pretended I wasn't bothered in the least about Daddy's absence. "Maybe he'll show up later," I said.

I gave Momma a hug and wished her a Merry Christmas. That cheered her up. "Merry Christmas, Pink," she said with a smile. (She'd called me Pinky since I was a baby.) Then she handed me a present. "Thank you, Momma!" I said. Then I carefully pulled off the bow and put it to the side so we could use it again next year. When I unwrapped the box, I was also careful not to tear the paper. I removed the top from the box and unfolded the tissue paper inside. But all I found was a small piece of paper with the word "sweater" written on it. I looked at Momma with a confused smile, searching for an explanation.

Momma began to cry again. "I didn't have enough money to buy you Christmas gifts this year, so this is what I would have gotten for you if I had the money." She went on to tell me that when she was able we would go to the store and pick up each gift written on the papers. "Really? Thank you, Momma!" I gave her another big hug. She handed me gift after gift. Inside each box was a small note that said, "shirt," then "jeans," "shoes," and so on. As I opened each gift, we talked excitedly about the style, color, and type of items I would eventually get. Then we lined up the papers into outfits: sweater with jeans, shirt with pants. In the end, Momma turned what could have been a holiday disaster into one of my best Christmases ever. Unfortunately, Daddy never did show up, not for Christmas or the week that followed.

# SEVEN

# OLYMPIC HOPEFUL

I turned sixteen in January of 1984. It was an Olympic year, and as an elite gymnast, it seemed like a golden opportunity. On the other hand, I had very little experience and recognition at this level, so the odds were against me. To qualify for Olympic Trials, I had to place in the top ten in the all-around competition at the American Classic, which was held in Minneapolis that year.

It was my first time competing at such a high level. I would be up against the likes of Tracey Talavera, Julianne McNamara, Kathy Johnson, and see coaches like Don Peters, Muriel and Abie Grossfeld, and Bela Karolyi, in action. Another gymnast I'd competed against was someone I had known for a year or so. Her former coach and my coach were friends, and she had come to my gym to train one summer. Now, she was at a new gym in Texas, training under Bela Karolyi. Her name was Mary Lou Retton. As you may already know, she went on to have a spectacular year, eventually winning gold in the 1984 Olympics. I had read about all of these people. Now we were going to be sharing the same apparatus and reaching into the same chalk bowl together. It was beyond anything I had imagined.

In the Classic, I competed well on beam, floor, and vault, making it into the top four. My final event was the uneven bars. To qualify for Olympic Trials, all I had to do was not fall. It seemed simple enough; the uneven bars were one of my best events. But I had one of the most difficult routines in the competition, which included three release moves. My first release was a reverse Hecht from a staldter position facing the low bar, a complicated move that started with a handstand on the high bar facing away from the low bar. Then I swung down and around the bar with my legs in a straddle position. As I came back up on the other side of the high bar, I let go. Then I threw myself into the air, whipped my upper body forward in the opposite direction, flipped over the bar, and caught it again. Don't sweat it if you can't picture this move in your mind. It is difficult to imagine if you've never seen the skill performed before.

This time, however, I misjudged my release. Before I knew it, I landed on my back on the high bar, bounced backward, and then fell headfirst onto the mat. I hit it so hard that when I opened my eyes I saw double. As I blinked at the ceiling, Jim appeared over me and whispered, "You better get up right now!" All I could think was, *This man is trying to kill me!* But I staggered over to the chalk bucket and tried to pull myself together. I wasn't even sure where I was, never mind what I was supposed to be doing. A few moments later, though, the judges came back into focus, and I suddenly remembered that this was the routine that would make or break my chances of going to the Olympic

Trials. So I got back up and continued my routine from where I left off.

I had been trained so well and practiced my routine so many times that even though I was in a state of shock, instinct took over. I caught my second release move and then my third. After that, all I had to do was a simple connecting skill, and then I was in the home stretch. By that time all I wanted to do was finish without falling again. It wasn't just fear of disappointment that drove me. I just didn't have it in me to climb back up a second time. Concentrating hard on technique and form, I left the low bar for the last time then kipped up to the high bar. I cast into a tight handstand, swung around, did a staldter to a handstand, and then another. I brought my toes to the bar for a toe-on front somersault with a half-twist dismount and … nailed it! I was so happy to finish strong like that.

I signaled the judges, who looked happy that I had recovered from the fall, then went over to my chair and began to loosen my handgrips. I slipped on my warm-up suit while eyeing the judges. "Please, God, let me make it," I prayed. The head judge motioned with her hand. The other three judges rose from their seats and walked over to the head judge's table for an impromptu conference. All I could do was wait.

Then the judges walked back to their seats, and the head judge quietly told my score to the score flasher. She put the numbers in one at a time, with the numbers facing away from us. Then she raised the pole and slowly rotated it in our direction. I knew that if I scored an 8.9 I would make it to Olympic Trials. As the pole turned toward me, that's exactly what I saw. As Jim congratulated me, I couldn't believe how happy I was to hug this man who had tortured me for so long. In that moment I couldn't thank him enough.

"Oh, and thank you, God," I whispered.

# EIGHT

# TWENTY-FOUR MAGICAL HOURS IN NEW YORK

Vidal Sassoon was one of the US National Team's sponsors in 1984. At the qualifying meet before Olympic Trials, his team gave all of us makeovers. Even though I was sixteen, that was the first time I had worn makeup. They took before and after photos. My transformation was so dramatic that they put my pictures in magazines and newspapers all over the country so they could show off this miracle they had just performed.

All of the attention led to an invite for Jim and me to appear on the *Today Show* with Bryant Gumbel, which was taped in New York City. In addition to me, they had invited another gymnast, Tracy Butler, and a diver and swimmer whose names I can't remember. They were also trying out for the Olympics. We got star treatment. They picked us up from the airport in a limousine and drove us to the Ritz Carlton Hotel, where I had my very own room.

Although I'd never been in a place as nice as the Ritz before, this was not my first time in a hotel. That happened several years earlier in a Ramada Inn. I was amazed to be in such a nice-looking room. It even came with an ice bucket, four drinking glasses, and a matching tray. When Momma unpacked my bags after the trip, she was horrified to discover I had brought the entire set home with me. I thought those items were complimentary. I would not make that mistake at the Ritz.

After a few moments to settle in, they whisked us off to Vidal Sassoon's salon. It was unlike anything I'd seen back home. A very nice woman hurried us in, saying, "Vidal is waiting for you!" *Vidal? Vidal himself?* Our faces revealed our surprise as we looked around at each other. Sure enough, there he was, in the flesh. He was a very handsome man, dressed casually, with perfect hair (of course). He was also very gracious and treated us like royalty.

His people proceeded to give us the works. We were pampered and groomed until we had "the look." To make a great story even greater, Vidal was the one who actually did my hair. He gave me a fabulous high-fashion cut and style. When he was finished, he ran his fingers through my hair several times then said in his English accent, "Shake it, dahling!" Afterward, we had a wonderful time talking about hair and makeup with the experts. As a gym rat from Cary Street, I needed all the help I could get.

Then it was time to go back to the hotel, where I ate dinner in the restaurant with the other three athletes. They told us to order whatever we wanted and then charge it to our rooms. I ordered the duck because it was the only thing on the menu I recognized. When the dust cleared, our bill came to eighty-four dollars between us. Even though Vidal was paying, I got a knot in my stomach when I saw the amount. I felt as though I had done something wrong. I looked around the restaurant to see if anyone knew we had just eaten eighty-four dollars worth of food. No one seemed to care. That amount of money would have supplied groceries at my house for over a month.

After signing our names and room numbers on the bill, we went back upstairs to get some rest. Not long after I got to my room, I heard a knock at my door. "Who is it?" I asked. A male voice with a thick accent responded, but I didn't understand what he said. The only man I knew with an accent was Vidal Sassoon. I thought he might be checking in with everyone to make sure all was well. "Vidal?" I asked. "Is that you?" The voice responded again, and I thought I heard the word yes. So I opened the door a crack, only to find one of the hotel workers standing there. "You're not Vidal!" I said.

"May I come in?" he asked.

"No!"

"I have a chocolate for you."

"I don't want your candy!" I slammed and locked the door. I knew the rule: "Never take candy from a stranger." I theorized the man had probably been watching me since dinner. He secretly followed me back to my room, and now he planned to break in and kill me. After putting a chair under the doorknob, just in case, I called Jim, who was just next door. "A hotel worker is trying to get me!" I said, my voice frantic with fear. By that time I was in tears. Jim assured me that everything was okay and that I had nothing to worry about. I hung up the phone, thinking he couldn't care less if I woke up dead. At least he could have offered to go out and search for the guy or call the police.

Only after many more hotel experiences did I realize that the poor gentlemen at my door was probably just there for the turn-down service, where they come into your room, turn down your bed covers, and leave a fancy chocolate on your pillow. I can laugh about it now, but can you blame me for responding the way I did? Just a few years earlier, the Atlanta child murders had put every black child I knew on edge. The Atlanta Child Murders were a series of killings committed between July 1979 and May 1981 that claimed the lives of over twenty black children. Candy or not, I was not going to be a victim of Charlie the Chocolate Bandit.

The next morning it was back to the salon to do our hair and makeup for the *Today Show*. After we were all made up, we were driven to Rockefeller Center where the show was being broadcasted. We all waited nervously in the small green room until it was time for our segment. Waiting along with us was a stunning black woman with the most beautiful dark eyes. Her name was Laura Carrington. Recently she had starred opposite Lionel Ritchie in his video for the song "Hello." Mr. Ritchie was also a guest on the show that day, and she was there to surprise him. She was very pleasant and engaging.

When it was our turn to go on, we walked out and took our place on the interview stools. In front of each stool was a "before" picture. Mine was absolutely awful. I was so embarrassed. Yes, millions of people would see my new coif created by Vidal himself. But they would also see the mess I was before he stepped into my life.

Before our segment, Bryant Gumbel tried to help us relax by making us laugh. He could sense the tension, I'm sure. Yes, we could flip across a four-inch piece of wood, dive from platforms several meters in the air, or swim with lightning speed, but sitting on a stool in front of millions of viewers, including my tenth grade biology class, was an altogether different kind of challenge. I wished Momma could have been watching, but she couldn't because of work. Despite my fears, the segment flew past without a hitch. Vidal went from athlete to athlete and explained how he and his team had taken us from blab to fab. When he was finished with me, he told me to "Shake it, dahling," which I did.

After the show, Bryant Gumbel let us take some photos with him. Lionel Ritchie also spent some time with us. Both men treated us so well. There was no pretense or disregard for us because they were celebrities and we were not.

As we walked back into the Ritz, I ran into Liza Minnelli, who was on her way out with two long racks of clothing on wheels. They were filled with beautiful show dresses with sparkles and fringes. I could just imagine her wearing them on stage. I asked for her autograph and was immediately caught off guard when she thanked me for asking. Here I found it an honor to meet her, but she acted as if it were an honor to meet me instead.

During my short stay in New York, I met several other celebrities and some very wealthy people. For some, the only way I knew they were celebrities was because my coach and others told me they were. I found it odd that none of them looked down on me. They all treated me with kindness and respect. Even though I was the only black person among the athletes and coaches, to them I was just like everyone else. Although the other girls were from a more affluent background than I was, the opulence to which we were exposed put all of us into a state of awe. It was so refreshing to not have to prove I was worthy to be in their presence.

Back home, people were so quick to look down on you for practically any reason at all. It could be because of the neighborhood in which you lived, the way you dressed, or the way you looked. If your skin was very dark, you were treated differently too. And if you were working hard to make a better life for yourself, they looked down on you because they thought you were trying to be someone you weren't, or worst of all, you were trying to be white. If anything, I expected even more of that type of treatment from the people I met in New York. But I experienced exactly the opposite. My background and the color of my skin didn't seem to matter.

# NINE

# OLYMPIC TRIALS ... AND TRIBULATIONS

I entered the Olympic Trials as a "rookie" elite, ranked number eight in the nation. Just one year before, I was the Junior Olympic National All-Around Champion. Now, I was vying for a spot on the Olympic team with elite veterans. To make it this far was impressive. I knew the meet was a big deal, but nothing prepared me for what I was about to experience. The Trials took place in Jacksonville, Florida. Along with the other athletes, I stayed in a spectacular condo unit located along a golf course. It was like something I had only seen on TV. Vidal Sassoon and his team were also there to do our hair and makeup. We traveled to and from the arena on big tour buses complete with a police escort to ensure we made it on time. Each time we got out of the bus there were television cameras and security guards everywhere. Our workouts were timed to the second to ensure everyone got a fair turn. When we weren't training we had to wear our credentials everywhere we went.

On the first day of competition, we did the required compulsory routines. According to Jim, I had a "gorgeous" performance on floor exercise. He was especially impressed with my front aerial, which had even garnered the praise of male Olympic gymnast Bart Conner. Jim described my bar routine as "awesome," and he commended me for my beautiful swing. I had a few more bobbles on beam than I'd hoped for, but my execution of the skills was a sight to see. I finished out the day with a good vault, and Jim was extremely proud of me.

Back at the condominium, I had hoped for a good night's sleep, yet my excitement and anticipation of the next day stole some of it away from me. The women's optional competition was *the* most popular event to watch. This is when we saw the spectacular tricks that displayed the fearlessness and originality of each athlete. I opened the event on floor exercise. It was one of my strengths, but I was up first, so my nerves were on edge. Just before I signaled the judges that I was ready to go, they told me to wait because we had to pause for a commercial break. The Trials were being broadcast live across the country, so the timing had to be perfect. The break took only a couple of minutes, but it felt like forever. As I jumped up and down and shook out my arms to get the blood flowing, I looked around at all the television cameras ready to capture my routine from every angle.

This was my first time participating in a televised competition. I felt more nervous than ever because I knew people at home would be watching. I didn't want to embarrass myself by making a mistake. I didn't want to go back to school and hear insensitive comments from my classmates who didn't understand the sport. I had always tried my best to fit in and not draw attention to myself. If I messed up on TV, they would surely talk about it, and I would no longer be able to fly under the radar. Finally the head judge raised her green flag, my signal to begin. I returned the signal with an arm wave and a nod and took the floor.

Everything went as planned during my routine. I was in great shape and was able to nail every tumbling pass, including my big finish, which was a double back. I signaled the judges when I was done and breathed a huge sigh of relief. It was a good start.

I was Jim's only athlete in the competition, so I had his undivided attention. The other gymnasts were from all over the nation. Many of them were also there without their teammates. Even though we were competing for the same spots, we cheered each other on. Most of us were friends both in and out of the gym, even though there were certain coaches who would not let their athletes fraternize with the "enemy," so to speak.

Next up was vault. Vault is the epitome of power, and it happens so quickly. One slip of the hand or a misaligned entry could ruin the whole performance. It was on this risky event that Diane Durham, the only other black gymnast in the competition and the favorite to win the Trials, injured herself. I was secretly rooting for her, and it was heartbreaking to witness her misfortune. She trained with Bela Karolyi and was poised to become America's sweetheart. I felt so badly for her because with this injury came shattered Olympic dreams.

The vault I competed was a handspring front tuck. On my first vault, I got a good push off the horse and plenty of height, but I misjudged my rotation and kicked out early, arching my back as my feet contacted the ground. I jarred my spine significantly, knocking the wind out of my lungs. After taking a few seconds to catch my breath, my first thought was whether or not I would be able to finish the competition. I still had a second vault to perform, but I wasn't even sure if I could go on.

Jim came over to see if I was okay. Because my landing looked so painful, he was immediately concerned about my back and wanted to buy time to give me rest and see if I could still compete. He was on a first name basis with all the judges, and he went to the head judge to see if we could have a little extra time before my next attempt. They were gracious and told us to take our time. Miraculously, at the same time, an assistant at the head table relayed a message from the TV truck that they were taking a commercial break and we had even *more* time for me to recover. Jim thought, *Thank you, Lord!* He knew that if my injury wasn't serious, I had another chance to deliver a great vault.

I was visibly shaken as the pain continued to pierce through my spine. The break, indeed, gave me enough time to get myself together. I made my way back to the end of the runway, but Jim was concerned that my confidence would wane. On the second vault, the pain taunted my body as I sprinted once again. It took everything I had to make it over that horse. My vault was higher than the first, but I kicked out too early again and sat down on my bottom. Jim was puzzled because it was unusual for me to miss two vaults in a row, but he was relieved that I wasn't seriously injured and proud of how aggressively I approached the second vault. I was so disappointed. I knew I might have just blown my chance to make the Olympic team. I still didn't give up hope, but now I would need to endure a tender spine for my final two events.

Next were the uneven bars. I had to pretend that vault never happened and focus on finishing the meet strong. While I was chalking up, an image of my fall on vault kept flashing through my mind. I had to literally shake my head to clear the picture and focus on the present.

While Jim set the bars, I double-checked the setting from the chalk tray. I had grown to be tall for a gymnast, and the bars had to be set at maximum height and width for my routines. Even at maximum settings, when I did a giant swing on the high bar, I still had to flex my feet so they would not hit the floor, and Jim still had to slide the landing mat away so my feet wouldn't hit that either. This had to be carefully choreographed because my score depended on it.

When my turn came, I mounted the bar with a simple kip double leg jam to the high bar. I watered down my routine by removing my first release move, the Tchachev (Remember the one on which I crashed at the American Classic, that left me seeing double?). I caught my first release move with an extra swing and did not perform my second one. Yet I worked to finish strong and swung nicely through the end of my routine. I got a quick, sympathetic handshake from Jim then went to prepare for the balance beam, my final event.

While waiting for my turn, I found a line on the floor to practice my routine. I winced on occasion as the movement of my body sent sharp pains through the bones in my spine. In between my skills I'd watch a competitor on beam. My muscles twitched with every one of her moves. If she wobbled to one side, I leaned in the opposite direction, as if it would help her to stay on the beam. When she finished her skill, I'd lift my head up as if to help her land. Finally, Jim had to get me to refocus on my own routine and warm up.

Even so, as I continued to practice, I kept sneaking glances at the other competitors' scores. It soon became clear that my routine would have to be extraordinary if I hoped to qualify for the Olympics.

With a lump in my throat, I lined up with the rest of the girls and made my way to the head judge's table. She greeted us with a smile and wished us luck. Before we competed, we had thirty seconds to warm up on the beam. It was only enough time to do a few choice skills. The judges were watching, so we had to be composed and give a good first impression.

I chose not to watch the girls who competed ahead of me. Instead, I spent my time visualizing a no-fall routine. If I saw someone else fall, I knew I would become more worried about my own ability to stay on the beam. And if I watched another girl do a great routine, then there would be even more pressure on me to do the same.

When it was my turn to compete, I set the springboard at the end of the beam then measured my steps perfectly so that I would not stutter step and miss my mount. I stood on my line marked with chalk, saluted the judge, and gazed at the end of the balance beam. I would need to hit the board straight and strong enough to do a front tuck somersault from the floor onto the beam. It was a blind landing, so even the slightest deviation on my takeoff could result in a fall.

I landed my mount with a bobble and executed my back handspring layout with the same unsteadiness. But with a deep breath and renewed focus, I nailed my front tuck and all of my required dance moves. My dismount was a back handspring double tuck. In the middle of my back handspring, I was slightly off center, and my hand slipped on the beam. In a split second, I had to choose whether I would go for my dismount anyway or play it safe and bailout. I chose to bail, and then I added a few dance moves to get myself back into position. Then I repeated the skill and landed my double back dismount, finishing strong. Although I finished without a fall, these mistakes further hurt my chances of making the team. I was not pleased with my performance, and I knew that the judges had not seen my best. But on beam, we only got one opportunity, and my fate was sealed.

We didn't officially find out who made the Olympic team until all four rotations were complete, but Jim knew right after my beam routine that I would not qualify. The elite veterans made fewer mistakes and had more difficulty in their routines. I was ignorant to this fact, so I held out hope. Once the totals were tallied, my beam score flashed above the judges' table.

Then it slowly rotated for all to see. When it finally turned toward me, my heart sank. It would not be good enough. Jim gave me a consoling hug on the shoulder. "Great job. You gave it all you had, and that is all we can expect from anyone." Jim knew I was disappointed, but he hoped that I would understand the bigger picture of what I had accomplished. Yet I wouldn't, until well into my adult years. Tears welled up in my eyes as I searched the stands for my parents. When I saw them, I could tell their hearts broke for me as well. This was my one big chance. I *could* try out for the Olympics again, but I would have to wait four long years.

# TEN

# THE AWAKENING

Failing to make the Olympic team was a huge disappointment, but I didn't have time to get mired in despair or regret. That's because the United States Gymnastics Federation selected me to represent the USA in the South African Cup. Together with a small team of male and female gymnasts, I would travel overseas to compete in two big meets. It would be the USA versus the RSA (Republic of South Africa).

In 1984, apartheid was still going strong in South Africa. I had seen news footage of the fighting and the terrible conditions under which black South Africans lived. But at the time, the idea of going over there to compete didn't strike me as controversial. Like Momma, I was just so excited about being selected for the team that the political implications of our trip didn't even cross my mind. And as an inquisitive sixteen-year-old, I was also curious to find out for myself what was really going on over there.

The flight to South Africa took over twenty hours, which included a brief refueling stop on a small desert island off the coast of Africa. When I left home, it was summertime. But when I stepped off the plane in

Johannesburg, I stepped straight into winter, the mildest winter I had ever seen.

Almost immediately, a group of reporters pulled Diane Durham, the other black gymnast, and me aside to take our pictures and ask us how we felt about competing there. I don't know about Diane, but this caught me completely by surprise. I didn't know how to answer their probing questions. But I could tell by the way the reporters acted that our presence there was a very big deal. All eyes would be on us wherever we went. For the first time I realized we were representing not only the US but also black people around the world.

After our impromptu press conference, we discovered that our luggage had failed to arrive. It was lost somewhere between the US and South Africa. While the airline attempted to track it down, the South African team was kind enough to lend us leotards so we could practice. I was thankful, until they handed me a tiny red and white outfit that looked as if it might fit a child's doll. Evidently, they had never seen a five-foot-seven gymnast before. All I can say is thank goodness for Lycra!

Some white South African families volunteered to let us live with them while we were in the country. The first home I stayed in was beautiful, with huge gardens in the backyard. After a brief tour, they showed my roommate, Dawna, and me to our room. Dawna trained away from home, so she was used to being gone from her family. But as we settled in, I began to feel homesick. I was excited to experience a new culture, but I didn't like being so far away from home. To help settle my mind, I pulled out my itinerary, which mapped out every practice and what we would be doing each day of the week. I visited those papers frequently throughout the rest of the trip, checking off each item as we completed it. Just seeing our progress encouraged me to keep going.

The next morning as we entered the kitchen for breakfast, I saw a black woman ironing clothes. She looked up at me with a surprised smile. The family introduced her as their ironing lady. She watched me as I took a seat at the table then went back to her ironing. Every now and then I would catch her glancing up at me with a slight smile on her face. She probably thought she would never see the day when a black person sat at this white family's table.

Through the kitchen's large picture window, I saw a black man working in the gardens. My host mother noticed that I kept watching him, so after breakfast she took me outside to meet him. He said a few words to her in Afrikaans. She laughed and turned to me. "He says he wants to marry you." They both chuckled at my surprised response. I just wanted to get out of there. The ironing lady and the gardener were domestic servants who likely lived on the property and away from their families. For black women in South Africa, being a domestic servant was often the only opportunity to work outside of the areas reserved for the black population. I've since read that being a domestic servant in South Africa during apartheid was tantamount to slavery because of the extremely long hours and the substantially low wages.

As we traveled back and forth to the gym each day, it was like stepping back in time. We drove past Soweto, which looked like it was on fire; there was smoke everywhere. These were the same townships I had seen on the news back in America, which were in the midst of violent unrest. When I asked about them, I was told that the smoke was from their chimneys. I did not believe it, though. I had already seen videos of the violence that was taking place. Seeing the thick clouds of smoke rise just several yards away only confirmed that the uprising was a reality. From then on, I was determined to keep my eyes and ears open.

---

On one of our afternoons off, we went to a shopping mall. As I walked past the various stores, I heard a beautiful, young, black South African woman call out. I looked around to see if she was talking to someone else but then realized she was talking to me. I waved to her and smiled.

As I stepped onto the escalator to go to the next floor, she called out again. I looked back and saw her pushing past several people on her way up the escalator. As she got closer to me, she said, "You're the American! You're the American!" When she finally reached me, she studied my face and smiled. She told me her name was Maggie. She said she had always dreamed of going to America, and she wanted to know if I could help her. I didn't know what I could do, but we exchanged addresses then went our separate ways.

I wandered through the mall until I reached a jewelry store. As I looked at some necklaces in a glass display counter, I noticed a black South African man cleaning nearby. When he drew close to me, I stepped aside so I wouldn't be in his way. But no matter how far I moved down the counter, he kept getting closer. Finally, he whispered, "You are American."

"Yes," I said as my eyes took in his tall, slender frame.

"Don't look at me," he said firmly.

Immediately, I dropped my head and pretended to look at the jewelry. He said that if he were caught talking with me, his life and the lives of his family members would be threatened. So we carried on a secret conversation without ever making eye contact. He told me his name was George and that he worked at the store as a custodian. Like Maggie, he wanted to leave South Africa, and he wanted me to help. He asked if we could exchange addresses. When I agreed, he disappeared for a few moments. While he was gone, I wrote my address on a small piece of paper and folded it up. He returned and started wiping the glass countertop with his dirty cloth. As subtle as a magician, he slid his address underneath my hand without missing a beat. As he continued to "clean the glass," I slipped my information under his cloth. Without a word, he took the note and disappeared.

Afterward, I went over to my teammates and told them what happened. The exchange was so clandestine that they didn't even notice it. These incidents made me even more determined to find out what was really happening in this country. I was amazed that the black people in this country were so desperate that they would turn to a sixteen-year-old girl for help. I had no idea what I could do for them, if anything, but I vowed to do whatever I could.

What they wanted most was for me to make contact with some of their associates in New York. Once I returned home, I tried to find these people, but as you can imagine it was extremely difficult and proved impossible for me to do. I knew that black South Africans were suffering, but I had no idea how bad it really was. It made me so thankful for the freedoms I took for granted back home. Even though America still had—and has—a long way to go in terms of race relations, the mere fact that I was in South Africa representing my country as a world-class athlete was proof that I had a life of incredible privilege compared to black people in this country.

My encounters in the mall continued to haunt me as we headed out to stay at a resort and go on a safari. My heart broke as we drove past shantytowns composed of countless shacks made from sheets of corrugated metal. Most of them looked like they couldn't even keep out the rain, much less house an entire family. The temperature inside those shacks at midday must have been unbearable. Not surprisingly, most of life carried on outdoors. People sat on rickety chairs, barrels, or whatever else they could find.

Despite the difficult conditions, as we drove past, the kids jumped up and down and ran alongside the bus, waving and smiling. I couldn't help but giggle at their expressions of joy. I placed my palm flat against the window until they were long out of sight. Then I sat back in my comfortable seat on the air-conditioned bus and cried. The white South Africans kept telling us that things weren't as bad for the black South Africans as the American press had led us to believe, but my experiences exposed the hollowness of those words.

I was not the only one on my team who was determined to learn more about the effects of apartheid. Two male gymnasts, both white, cared almost as much about the issue as I did. We talked frequently about the injustices and how we wanted to know more. We had been well versed in the white perspective. Now we wanted to hear what the black South Africans had to say.

At the resort, we asked a number of the black workers if they would give us the inside scoop, but they responded to us as if we had the plague. No doubt, they also feared for their jobs and their safety. But we were young, stubborn, and not easily discouraged. Finally, we found a worker who was willing to talk. He told us to meet him on the rooftop that evening. We were so excited as we went back to hang out with our teammates, but we didn't dare let anyone else know what was up.

When the time for our meeting arrived, the three of us slipped away one by one so no one would notice. Then we rendezvoused at a fire escape and climbed up to the roof. Our new friend was right there waiting for us. He started out by making it clear that we were to tell no one we had talked. He would not even tell us his name. He said that if he were caught sharing this information with Americans, he would be killed.

We sat for some time, listening in amazement as he told us of the hardships his people faced. The denial of rights, substandard living conditions, and inhumane treatment were among their concerns. There were laws that dictated where they were allowed to go, what they were allowed to do, and when they were allowed to do it. The apartheid system destroyed the black families by separating men from their families and even mothers from their children. The demeaning conditions in which they lived made it seem as if they were less than human, of no value unless they could provide menial labor. Even then, they were subjected to poor wages and garnered no real respect.

The three of us were outraged, but we also felt helpless. What could we do? But the man's testimony also hit me at a deeper level. If I had grown up in South Africa, I would have fallen under the same rules. My dreams and my ability to succeed in life would have been denied because of the color of my skin. I realized that this was the same pain my parents felt when they were discriminated against each day while growing up, the same pain my father felt while in the US Army, the same pain my grandmother felt as she served in the homes of rich white families because no other options were available.

The worker told us his people were hurting, but they were also angry and ready to fight back. They were even training an army of Zulu warriors who would fight for equality. "It is almost time," he said with hope in his eyes. He was one of those warriors. There was not a drop of shame in his body, only fire and hope for a different tomorrow. It was overwhelming to know that we had information that was not even known to most South African citizens.

As I wandered around the resort afterward, I looked at the black workers with newfound empathy. I decided I would make an effort to touch each one of them, whether it was with a smile, a compliment, or an encouraging word. I picked a beautiful flower from a garden and presented it to a black South African woman who had clearly worked many hours and was tired from the day. "This is for you, a beautiful flower for a beautiful woman," I said. She laughed as if I were joking. But when she saw I was serious, she thanked me and lifted the flower to her nose so she could inhale its rich scent. As I watched, the color of the flower cast a reflective glow upon her perspiring face. Then she hid the flower in her clothing and got back to work, but not before flashing me another grateful smile.

We didn't tell anyone else about our little meeting until we were safely away from the resort. Even then, we made sure our tour guides didn't overhear us. We didn't want word to get back to the resort that the Americans had been talking with the black staff, for fear of what would happen to them.

―――――

Of course, we didn't spend all of our time in South Africa investigating apartheid. We were there to compete, so that's what we did in both Pretoria and Johannesburg. The United States Gymnastics Federation expected us to go in and win the competitions no matter what the conditions were for black people in South Africa. The biggest challenge for me was some of the equipment. It was quite different from what I used at home, especially the uneven bars and the springboard for vault. The springboard was much harder than what I was used to, so I had to hit it with more power to get the required bounce. But the most difficult adjustment was the balance beam. Their beams were very slippery, which meant that if I were off even a little bit in my landing, I would slip and fall. Despite these setbacks, our team was able to make the necessary adjustments, to the point where we won the first competition.

While training for our second competition, I was sitting off to the side putting on my beam shoes when I glanced up and saw a large group of young black people sitting in the stands. They looked like college students. At that moment I felt such a strong sense of kinship with them. Even though we were from different countries, we had so much in common. As I smiled and waved at them, I wondered if they were even allowed to use the facility in which I was competing. Were they sitting so far back in the stands because they weren't allowed to sit near the front? Would I have even been allowed to compete if I were born in South Africa instead of America? Or would I be like them, relegated to watching from the sidelines?

Such thoughts inspired me to represent my country well. As I warmed up for the competition, I had an insatiable drive to win, more powerful than I'd ever felt before.

I felt pretty good throughout the meet until it came time to do my final event, the dreaded balance beam. The scene reminded me of my experience at the Olympic Trials. There was no room for butterflies or hesitation. I needed to perform my routine with confidence so I could finish the meet strong. If I did, there was a chance I would win the all-around medal.

Once I mounted the beam, there was no looking back. As I moved through my routine, I was very conscious of the audience watching me. Most likely, they were all keeping track of the scores, and they knew exactly what score I needed to win the meet. As I set up for my dismount, I pushed such thoughts from my mind. I had to focus. A few steps and ... applause filled the room. I had nailed it!

When the score was flashed, it became apparent to all that a black woman had just won the South African Cup. I was filled with joy as I put on my warm-ups. "I did it! Thank you, God! I did it!"

Chills shot up my spine during the awards ceremony as they gave out the medals for second and third place. Finally, they announced my name as the all-around winner. What a feeling. I congratulated the other winners before taking my spot on the podium.

As I turned to face the audience, I noticed a commotion in the stands. After all I had learned of this country, I was a bit scared because I knew it was possible that many white South Africans were upset I was even allowed to compete in the event, much less win it all. Then I realized it was merely audience members and the press clamoring to get pictures of this historic moment.

As the cameras flashed, thoughts of what I had experienced in such a few short weeks flooded my mind. I had performed better than every girl on South Africa's national team, even though all of them were white. When they placed the gold medal around my neck and handed me a large bouquet of red roses, I glanced instinctively toward the spot where I had seen the black South African students earlier. *This is for you*, I thought. I waved my hand and looked around at the sea of white faces, all of them cheering for me, a black girl, from Richmond, Virginia. I only hoped that this small victory would help prove that blacks and whites *are* equal. Given the same opportunity, all of us can flourish in our God-given gifts.

I have no regrets about going to South Africa, even though in retrospect it was not the "politically correct" thing to do. In 1982 the UN, in its condemnation of apartheid, had called for sanctions against South Africa. Because I competed there in 1984, I was placed on the UN's blacklist. Still, I got to witness firsthand what was really going on over there, and it gave me a new sense of appreciation for my life back in America, as difficult as it was. It also gave me such a love for the African people—my people. I would never be the same.

On the flight home, I was finally able to relax, the pressure of the meets behind me. I couldn't help but replay all that had happened during the trip. My eyes welled with tears at the memory of a black South African woman cleaning up the gym where we practiced. When I returned to the United States, I would be cleaning the gym too. But at least I also had the privilege of using it. Did she have a little girl at home who was gifted in gymnastics and was teaching herself how to do various moves on the sidewalk? Would her talent ever be discovered? Would she be given the opportunity I had to develop into a world-class gymnast? Most likely, the answer was no. Yet we were the same. The only difference was opportunity. As I had sung so many times on those long walks home, I thought, *Let us march on 'til victory is won.*

# ELEVEN

# BACK TO REALITY

Competing in high-profile national and international meets gave me quite a bit of recognition on television and in the press. They called me the "sidewalk gymnast" because of how I first learned to tumble. I was in the newspaper quite often, and I was featured on the local news channels and in a commercial for our gym. Once, I was even invited by Lynda Bird Johnson-Robb, eldest daughter of Lyndon B. Johnson, to attend a function supporting the Ronald McDonald house. She was the wife of then governor Chuck Robb, so media coverage of the event was quite extensive. Every couple of weeks Richmond's school superintendent, Dr. Richard Hunter, sent us copies of news articles written about me, each one accompanied by a personal note of congratulations. This really made me feel special. The entire city and the state rallied behind me. I didn't care for all the attention, though, because I was still pretty shy.

After returning home from South Africa, I went to visit my Grandma Justine. Gymnastics was the furthest thing from my mind at that point. I was just glad to be home and away from all the pressure. I barely had a chance to sit down, though, when my mean cousin put her face in mine and said with a scowl, "You ain't nobody. You're just like everybody else. So don't think you're gonna be treated special around here." I don't know what had been said about me before I arrived, but obviously she thought I needed a reality check. Thankfully, my other family members were very supportive and encouraging. By the way, today I have a great relationship with my "mean" cousin. I love her dearly, and I know she loves me too.

Frequently I had to deal with family members who made fun of the way I spoke in the media. If I used proper English, they said I was trying to be white. When I did interviews on television, they would watch and then mock the way I talked. My grandmother on my father's side even called me her "white grandchild." She said I had forgotten where I came from. All I could think was, *How could I forget where I came from? I'm still here!* They didn't understand that I spoke proper English at the gym simply so there would be one less difference between my teammates and me. I also spoke proper English in my television interviews because I had seen other black athletes who did not and was embarrassed by them. To me, their speech made them appear less intelligent, which fed into the stereotype of black people being intellectually inferior. It was a challenge making sure my proper English didn't slip out at the wrong times, around my family. I had to become, as I've heard Will Smith say, "bi-dialectic."

With all of my recent successes, you'd think I would have developed a hint of arrogance and a sense of entitlement. Yet somehow I felt more humble and appreciative of my circumstances than ever before. I went away to the continent of my ancestors with a nonchalant attitude toward my existence, but I returned with a sense that my life was more than just a random series of events. Rather than feeling entitled, I felt humbled by the tremendous influence and responsibility I had as a public figure. I was determined to make the most of it.

There was a reason I had been given this talent, a reason my skin was not white but brown, and a reason my family struggled so much to make ends meet. If I were a white gymnast with means, maybe it would have been a little easier for me to accomplish my goals. But would my life have had the same impact on others? By following my dream, I realized I was inspiring others to do the same. Even adults approached me to say how much my example meant to them. So even though I was back to reality, my view of that reality would never be the same.

Despite all of the excitement and acclaim that came along with being a world-class gymnast, by age sixteen, I was craving a normal life. My social activities were pretty much limited to my school day, the gym, and an occasional slumber party with my gymnastics friends. On the rare weekend when I was at home, I spent my Friday and Saturday nights listening to music and dancing by myself in the living room. My tiny music collection consisted of Prince, Michael Jackson, and the Sugar Hill Gang. Once, I choreographed an entire production to every single song on Prince's *Purple Rain* album. I was tired of being alone, and I wanted to go out with friends and have fun, like my peers at school were doing.

My best friend was Robin. She was an honor student like me, so most of our classes were together. I think we hit it off because we loved to be different from everyone else. We didn't like drama, and we purposely went against the flow when it came to fashion. Everywhere we went, laughter followed, and we were always up to something. We were the black Lucy and Ethel, Thelma and Louise, and we were inseparable.

Around this time I went to my first party. It took place on the other side of town in an area called Church Hill. Momma was kind enough to drive Robin and me there in Grandma Esther's yellow Ford Pinto, which she had loaned to us so that Momma and Daddy could get to work.

As we pulled up, the party was already in full swing. The music was loud, and dozens of teenagers overflowed onto the streets. We didn't see anyone we knew, and the scene looked a bit intimidating, but we jumped out of the car anyway, eager to put some distance between ourselves and Momma. She promised to pick us up at 4:00 a.m. sharp.

We made our way inside, squeezing past people who danced in unison and chanted their mottos and cheers. They went back and forth trying to upstage each other. In some of the Richmond high schools, a Greek system was developed that was similar to the sororities and fraternities on college campuses. I was a member of Sigma Xi Omega. Our colors were pink and baby blue.

Our frat brothers, who attended a school across town, were also Sigmas, only they wore blue and white. The majority of them lived in Church Hill, and we were in their territory. Robin and I worked our way up against a wall to keep from being pushed and shoved. As I watched the crowd bounce to the music, I could feel the bass vibrating my bones as I stood against the wall. Every now and then guys would come up and ask us to dance. We usually obliged, but even when we didn't have partners, we danced anyway.

Suddenly a chorus of male voices cut through the air as a line of guys in blue sweatshirts with white lettering wove their way through the crowd. They chanted their song and stepped in unison, grabbing everyone's attention. These were our fraternity brothers, the Sigmas. One of their members, whose sweater said "Mr. B." on the back, caught my attention. We exchanged numbers later that night, and he became my first "real" boyfriend. I had a "so-called" boyfriend before. He was the son of the drug dealer who lived next door to Grandma Justine. We were only thirteen, and it didn't last long because he ended up going to jail for shooting somebody, so I don't count him.

At 4:00 a.m. on the dot, we went outside. We dared not be late, or else Momma would come into the party looking for us, which would embarrass us to no end. We strolled outside and pretended we were just hanging out. After making sure no one was watching, we dashed to the yellow Pinto and jumped inside. I begged Momma to pull away before anyone saw us. Once we were out of the sight, I relaxed and told her how much fun we had. This marked the beginning of a new era for me. No longer would my social life be limited to a smelly gym or dancing alone at home on the weekends. I had attained a hint of normalcy at last.

Once word got around that I could go out, my friends at school began to invite me to go places with them. I was always very excited to be included. One night when I came downstairs dressed to go out with friends, I found Daddy and his cousin at the kitchen table with a *huge* pile of marijuana. I paused briefly to watch as they de-seeded it by holding an album cover at an angle and then letting the herb slide down it. The seeds rolled down onto the table while the herb stuck to the album. When they were done, they separated the herb into little baggies.

*Why now?* I thought. My friend was about to arrive any minute, but my father's little drug operation was in full view of the front door. I ran upstairs and asked Momma to tell Daddy to put the drugs away before my company arrived. Then, just in case he refused, I went back down and waited by the door. My plan was to open it just wide enough to squeeze through without my date being able to see into the kitchen. I waited anxiously for several minutes. Then I remembered I had forgotten something upstairs. During the ten seconds it took me to run up and get it, my friend showed up. I rushed back downstairs to find him in the living room saying hello to Daddy. I said a quick hi and then hurried him out the door, hoping he hadn't seen the pile of pot in the kitchen.

When we got into his car, I looked straight ahead and acted as if nothing had happened. But he just stared at me with a shocked look on his face. I tried to initiate a conversation, but he didn't respond. Finally, I said, "What?" He just laughed and said, "Man, your dad is about to get blowwwed!" I smiled to cover my shame, thinking, *I can't believe this is happening.*

It ended up becoming a joke at school among a few of my friends. If anyone wanted to get high, they could just go to my house. I tried to laugh it off. But they had no idea how my father's drug use affected our family. They didn't understand what it was like to wait in fear for their father to come home, not knowing what state of mind he would be in. We never really talked about our home lives with each other, so my peers just assumed that because I was a gymnast who did lots of traveling, I came from a typical middle-class family. They didn't know the heartache my momma went through or about my father's no-shows at Thanksgiving and Christmas. They didn't know how the drugs affected his ability to remember our special moments together, moments that meant so much to me. Few people knew about that side of my life before that night.

Although I was surrounded by marijuana as a teenager, I didn't smoke it, though I had experimented with it when I was younger. One night I was "kicking it" with some new friends in a downtown parking lot when someone pulled out some weed. I just stood there talking and laughing as they lit up. Then, on impulse, I grabbed the rolling paper and rolled a joint. It took all of them by surprise. What did I, a world-class gymnast, know about rolling joints? My reputation to them was somewhat on the square side. One of the guys insisted on knowing how I had learned my technique. I merely shrugged and said, "I just know." When they kept pressing me about my unexpected knowledge, I decided to take things a step further and show them I knew all the ins and outs of smoking it too. I did it because I was tired of being thought of as an outsider. It wasn't that I wanted get high. I guess I just wanted to be "normal," whatever *that* was. I didn't think about how it would affect my body or my gymnastics career. At that moment, my need to be accepted meant more.

I don't know if this newfound knowledge about me was ever shared with others. If it was, I never heard about it. At school I was still "Kim the gymnast," "Flip," or "Superstar." My new reality had evolved into a life of trying to fit in with whatever situation presented itself. A better nickname would probably have been "Kim the Chameleon."

Momma and Daddy.

Grandma Justine and me on the back
porch of the house in "The Bottom."

Kissing Daddy in Germany, 1970, age two.

At the park with Momma in Germany, 1971, age three.

My third birthday, Germany 1971.

Momma, Daddy, Kizzie, and me.

Scared of doing a new trick (Valdez) on
beam, June 1979, age eleven.

Celebrating a win at state meet with
my Class II teammates and Coach Judy Shaw.

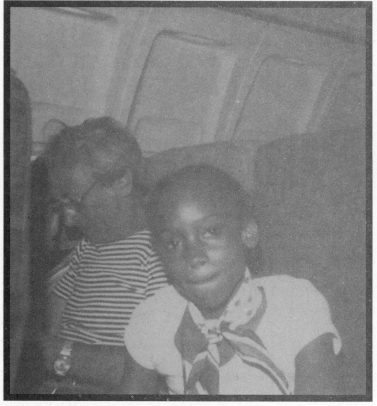

On my way to Bermuda at age eleven—
notice the hiding of the lips.

Posing in front of my trophies, trying to hide
my lips again, June 1983, age fifteen.

Muffie, Julie, Kendra, and I enjoy a snack after a meet.

Warming up before ballet class, 1983, age fifteen.

Uneven bars, From the Richmond Times Dispatch,
March 16, 1984, photo by Masaaki Okada.
Reprinted by permission.

"Before and After" photos for Vidal Sassoon, 1984.

Getting pointers from my coach, Jim,
during competition in London.
Photo by Eileen Langsley/International
Gymnast Magazine.

Celebrating the win on floor exercise at the Coca-Cola
Invitational in London, England, fall of 1984.
To my right is Romanian Cristina Grigoras, member
of 1984 Olympic Gold Medal Team. To my left is Great
Britain's Sally Larner, an '84 Olympian as well.

Balance beam.

Me at UCLA, 1987.

Corwin and me after winning my second floor
exercise title at Nationals in Utah, 1988.

Warming up on bars at UCLA, 1988.

With Momma during summer break from UCLA, 1989.

Covering a gymnastics meet for ESPN, 2000.
Photo by Steve Lange. Reprinted with permission.

Speech at Hall of Fame induction ceremony, 2000.

With the Dungys at the Super Bowl Breakfast, 2009.

With Momma and Daddy, May 2009.

# COLLEGE? ME?

When my junior year came around, my coaches started talking to me about college. They spoke of the need for me to begin thinking about what college I wanted to attend. As unbelievable as it may sound, I knew next to nothing about college. I had heard kids talk about it at school. I knew of one cousin who graduated from college, and my cousin Donna was in her second year, but they came from "true" and steady two-parent households, where their fathers had stable jobs and they owned their own homes. They didn't have to live at Grandma's off and on to avoid being homeless or endure the unstable home environment that I did. Subsequently, I didn't think college was a real possibility for *me*. Momma never talked about me pursuing an education past high school. So at that point in my life, there was no real motivation.

It wasn't until twenty years after I graduated from high school that Momma explained why she never encouraged me to go to college. When she was in high school, she did very well academically. She was even part of the National Honor Society. Her good grades earned her a full scholarship to Virginia State University in

Petersburg and Virginia Union University in Richmond. But because her parents could not afford the twenty-five dollar application fee, she was not able to take advantage of the opportunity. That may seem like a small amount of money, but it was impossible to come by for her family. And in those days, you didn't borrow money you couldn't pay back. It was devastating for Momma.

Her disappointment still held her captive many years later when it came time for me to decide whether or not to continue my education. She thought the only way to protect me from the same type of disappointment was to not even mention the possibility. My coaches kept telling her I could go to college on a gymnastics scholarship, possibly at one of the top schools in the nation, but she could not fathom the idea. Thankfully, they persisted, and Momma agreed to at least explore the opportunity.

To our surprise and delight, when recruiting season arrived, many top colleges invited me to become a part of their program. The attention was almost overwhelming. It didn't take me long to decide where I wanted to go. From the time I was in elementary school, I had an affinity toward UCLA, even though I had no idea where UCLA was. I was particularly impressed with UCLA's basketball coach, John Wooden, and what he had done with their team. I had watched them win a national championship in the 1970s, and from that moment I knew I wanted to go to that school. Even so, I decided to take a few other recruiting trips just to be safe. After my first three trips, however, my childhood aspirations to become a UCLA Bruin still held strong, so I decided to accept their offer of a full scholarship.

Initially, when I told my school guidance counselor that I wanted to apply to UCLA, he said I should consider applying to some local schools instead. I told him I didn't want to go to a local school; I wanted to go to UCLA. As I handed him the application form, which I had already filled out, it was clear he was perturbed by my insistence.

A couple of weeks later, the head gymnastics coach from UCLA called to say they hadn't received my application yet. Had I changed my mind? I went back to my guidance counselor to make sure he had sent it in. He insisted that he did, but then a week later I received an acceptance letter from a different California school. As it turns out, my counselor had sent my application to the wrong place, in spite of my scholarship to UCLA. Perhaps he wasn't diligent because he believed it was impossible for one of his students to attend such a prestigious university on the west coast. Coming from a predominantly black public school, I wondered if this white counselor's expectations for me were not very high. It saddens me to think of all the other students who may have been limited by the low expectations of counselors and teachers but had no one to intervene on their behalf. In my case, I called my future coach and told him what was going on. He tracked down my application, rerouted it to UCLA and I was accepted in 1986.

With my post-secondary plans secure, my senior year should have been a breeze. Instead, it was very difficult. I continued to struggle with problems at home, particularly my growing animosity toward Daddy. The older I got, the more aware I became of the hurt and pain he had caused our family. He stayed away from home more often now, and when he did come home, Momma and I always ended up in tears. He verbally ripped us apart with his criticism. We could do *nothing* to make him happy. We hardly ever had meat in the refrigerator because we couldn't afford it. For even this, he would yell and get *so* angry because he had to come home to nothing to eat. Momma was doing everything she could to meet our needs, but her best just wasn't good enough. As life grew more intense, I reached a point where it was difficult to concentrate on my sport. After eight years of competition, my mind was weary and my body was weak.

Suddenly I became very rebellious, and I didn't care about gymnastics anymore. I just wanted a break. I began to skip practice and hang out late at night with my friends. My coaches expressed their concerns to Momma, and she approached me about the issue. I told her I was tired and didn't want to do gymnastics anymore. I didn't want to go to college either. She listened to my thoughts and created a welcoming environment for me to vent about my feelings and frustrations. Then she suggested that I attempt to make it through the final months of training at Richmond Olympiad and try UCLA out for one week. If I liked it, I could stay. If I didn't, I was free to come home and end my gymnastics career. I thought this was a good compromise, and I agreed to the plan.

During this time, I became engrossed in movies that were full of violence and death. I practiced the fighting skills my daddy had taught me, and I imagined myself taking the life of another person. My heart became very hard, and I didn't care about anyone, not even myself.

Secretly, I thought that perhaps death would bring the peace that I longed to have. No more practice, no more pain. No more expectations. *No more pressure.* I had prayed many times for God to help me when I was in need, but it became harder and harder to do. Was he even there, or had I just been wasting my time waiting for him to fix my life?

I had absolutely no motivation to do anything. Knowing that others would find it difficult to understand, I kept my feelings to myself. But as much as I tried to stuff them down, they continued to ooze out through my poor decision-making and the way I was neglecting my gymnastics career. Every once in a while I'd pick up my kiddy Bible and thumb through it. I knew I needed help, but I didn't know where to turn. So I just slept with it in my arms, thinking maybe that would bring me the comfort I needed.

The closer I got to my departure date for UCLA, the more frightened I became. During my years of international travel, I was always prone to homesickness, even if the trip was only for a week or so. This time I'd be flying three thousand miles away to start an entirely new life, and I had no idea when I'd be back. How ironic that I was afraid to leave the chaos of my home life to move on to bigger and better things. I guess we all, at times, cling to what is familiar, no matter how miserable it may be. How was I going to make it? Would I struggle to fit in again? Would Momma be okay without me? I knew there was only one way to answer these questions: by taking a leap of faith.

My uncle Vernon (Grandpa Raymond's brother) and aunt Ruth gave me a going-away party. They were so proud of me. My cousins, aunts, and uncles on my father's side were all there. I received a few presents, but the one that stood out the most was a Bible from Aunt Ruth and Uncle Vernon. It was white with my name engraved in gold on the front. Inside, Aunt Ruth had marked Psalm 121.

> I will lift up my eyes to the mountains; from where shall my help come? My help comes from the Lord, who made heaven and earth. He will not allow your foot to slip; he who keeps you will not slumber. Behold, He who keeps Israel will neither slumber nor sleep. The Lord is your keeper; the Lord is your shade on your right hand. The sun will not smite you by day, nor the moon by night. The Lord will protect you from all evil; he will keep your soul. The Lord will guard your going out and your coming in from this time forth and forever.

These words lifted my heart and calmed some of my fears. I had no idea how much I would come to rely on them over the next few months and years as I struggled to make sense of my life.

## THIRTEEN
# A NEW LIFE BEGINS

In the summer of 1986, I landed at LAX to report for early training. My new head coach, Jerry Tomlinson, picked me up. I first met him when I competed for the US national team in a meet against China. I was about seventeen at the time, and we competed in the LA Forum, where the Lakers played. We even got to use their locker room to prepare for the meet. As a Lakers fan, it was exciting to see the lockers of Kareem, Magic, Worthy, and Byron Scott and to compete where they played their home games.

After the competition, I went over to the audience to sign autographs. That's when Jerry introduced himself. He told me that he was the head gymnastics coach at UCLA and that he wanted me to come to his school. He wasn't pushy. He spoke in a matter-of-fact kind of way. But since I wasn't even thinking about college, his words caught me totally off guard. *He must be some nutcase,* I told myself, *some weird guy who is a huge gymnastics fan trying to make conversation.* So I merely smiled, nodded, and then quickly moved on. Now, little more than a year later, that "nutcase" was picking me up from the airport. Of course, Jerry wasn't nutty at all. He was a happy guy with curly blond hair. He was excited to have me in his program, and he tried his best to make me feel at home. I enjoyed his demeanor and was happy to have someone like him coaching me.

As we drove to the UCLA campus, he pointed out all the famous places and told me the history behind them. I couldn't believe I was attending a school in such proximity to Bel Air, Beverly Hills, Brentwood, and Hollywood, where so many famous people lived.

At one point we stopped at a convenience store so I could call Momma on a payphone to let her know that I had arrived safely. When she asked me where I was, I looked around for a sign, and the first one I saw said "Liquor." So I told her we were at a liquor store (pronounced "licka stow"). Jerry was quite embarrassed because it sounded as if he had convinced my mother to let her baby go all the way to Los Angeles, assuring her that he'd take good care of me, and then the first place he took me was to the "licka stow." He didn't realize that Momma wasn't fazed by it at all. Neither was I. I'd spent a lot of time with my aunt Lois in the "licka stow" when I was little.

When we finally arrived on campus, its beauty blew me away. The sun, the palm trees—it was a dream come true. I noticed that many of the other students were driving shiny new cars, probably graduation presents. The cars weren't just new either. They were top-of-the-line luxury models. I had definitely entered a different world.

As we drove around the campus, my coach pointed out the bookstore. Seeing as I was on full scholarship,

I thought they would give me a voucher to purchase textbooks. But he told me the scholarship covered my tuition, room and board only. Textbooks would have to come out of my own pocket. I was shocked. All the other schools had offered a true full scholarship. When I signed with UCLA, I thought I was getting the same deal. In fact, I was so certain books were included that when I won $150 from an essay contest toward the end of my senior year, I used the money to buy sheets, a comforter, and other supplies rather than save it for books. So even before I actually set my foot on the campus grounds, my excitement about this new venture began to dim somewhat. Here I was in a school where students drove luxury cars, and I couldn't even pay for my own books.

Jerry spoke so bluntly about me having to pay for my books that I felt awkward pushing the matter any further. It was if he had told me this was the case, but I didn't remember it being so at all. Had I known, I would have had to choose one of the other colleges that would have covered *all* of my expenses. I sure could have used a mentor or someone else who knew the ins and outs of the recruiting process and what to look for when choosing a school. Neither Momma nor I really understood it, and there was no one in our lives to counsel us so that we could avoid situations like this one. Pensively, I sat back in my seat hoping that somehow Momma would be able to come up with more money to cover this new expense.

Jerry dropped me off in front of my dorm, where the other students were waiting in line with their parents. That's when the first twinge of loneliness set in. I missed my mother and wished she could be there to help me move in. The other students had refrigerators, televisions, stereos, and all the other "necessities" of college life. I made my way through the line with nothing more than a suitcase and a duffle bag. I also had yet to see anyone else with brown skin like me. When I reached my room, I was disappointed to discover it was nothing more than a small rectangular box with cold, empty cement walls. I sat down on my bed and began to cry. "Oh, God, please help me. I want to go home." Everything screamed that I did not belong.

I did a lot more crying over the next few days. But every day I opened my new Bible to the passage Aunt Ruth had marked: "I will lift up mine eyes unto the hills, from whence cometh my help. My help cometh from the LORD, which made heaven and earth."

My loneliness was compounded by the fact that I was quite shy, which made it difficult to make friends. A few students reached out to me, but I preferred to stay in my room. For a while I would only venture out for gymnastics practice and meals.

On my first day of practice, I walked into the Wooden Center and saw another black student for the first time. Where I grew up, you said hello to people when you passed by them. And because she was wearing a shirt of the sorority I had been invited to pledge while I was a high school senior on the east coast, I was all the more confident she would be a friend and not a foe. Boy, was I wrong. When I said hello, she merely looked me up and down, rolled her eyes, and refused to respond. She walked right past me as if I wasn't there. I was so shocked and angered that I refused to pledge that sorority even when they invited me to do so a couple of years later. Her reaction led me to believe that this organization didn't truly represent all that I had been told about them. This experience discouraged me all the more, so I continued to leave my room only when necessary.

It was so ironic. Here I was on this beautiful campus, surrounded by opportunity, but I was too depressed to take advantage of it. I think I was simply burned out. I called Momma and said I wanted to come home, but she convinced me to try it for another week. If I still didn't like it, I could leave. Deep inside, I knew that giving up and going home would mean sacrificing the opportunity of a lifetime. If I could just push through, perhaps I could overcome my homesickness and maybe even learn a thing or two.

At freshman orientation, I sat in a large auditorium where they prepped around five hundred students on what college life required from us. I was one of the few black students peppered throughout the "sea of salt." They had us look at the student to our left and the student to our right. Then they let us know that one of those students would not be there in the future. They would either fail out or bail out for various reasons. By the end of the orientation, I was sure that I'd be one of those who bailed.

As freshman athletes, we had an additional orientation. In a relatively small room in the athletic department, some of the best freshmen athletes in the nation and from every sport gathered. We learned about the John Wooden pyramid of success. Yes, John Wooden, that basketball coach from the seventies, who was partially responsible for me desiring to attend the university. A tradition UCLA athletics followed for every orientation was to bring back a former UCLA athlete to be the keynote speaker. This year, whom would they have but the Los Angeles Lakers' Kareem Abdul-Jabbar. I was on cloud nine. He walked in and stood before us. His seven-foot, two-inch frame towered above me as I sat on the second row. I listened to his every word as he recounted his years at UCLA and encouraged us in our academics as well as athletics. *What have I gotten myself into? This is big. Really big!* I thought to myself. From that moment on, I knew I would brave the next four years with tenacity. Whatever my situation, I would strive to live up to the call placed upon every UCLA recruit.

Some of the classes at UCLA were enormous. They had up to five hundred students. It was impossible for the professor to take attendance, so it was tempting to skip class. Some professors had accents so strong that I had to record their voices and replay the tape over and over again to decipher their words. Others spoke so quickly that I couldn't take notes fast enough. As athletes, we were required to attend study hall and were given tutors to help us stay on track academically. I was extremely thankful for this because without a tutor, there was no way I would have passed some of those classes.

My college workouts were quite different from the way we did things back in Richmond. At UCLA we only trained four hours per day. That was the limit placed on us by the NCAA. Our workouts were similar to the ones at home, in that we trained on each event daily. However, in college the repetitions decreased significantly. Instead of fifteen no-fall beam routines in a row, we did five. On bars, we knocked out three routines, and on floor, we did a workout that increased our endurance without pounding our bodies too much. When we practiced vault, we landed in the pit (similar to an in-ground swimming pool but filled with foam blocks instead of water) or a platform of mats built on top of the pit, which mimicked what we landed on in competition. This made for a nice, cushy landing and saved our knees and ankles. This lighter workout schedule also proved to be a lot easier on my body, which was a benefit when it came to my competitions.

After working out in the gym, we'd walk past Pauley Pavilion and into the weight room we shared with the other athletes. Then we went upstairs to the training room to take care of our aches and pains. I iced my ankles in the whirlpool and got therapy on other aching body parts. If I didn't have time to stay, I ordered my ice to go. Then I would hike up the hill to my dorm with ice wrapped tightly against my ankles, knees, shoulder, back, or whatever other body part ailed me that day. Sometimes I would not make it back up the hill in time for dinner, and I'd have to go hungry for the rest of the night.

While no one was allowed to watch us practice back home, our gym inside the John Wooden Center was like a fishbowl. Anyone could watch us through the huge two-story glass windows that surrounded our workout space. One day as I was trying to get through the day's assignments on balance beam, I turned toward the window to do a split jump, and lo and behold, there was Magic Johnson. Only this time it wasn't my imagination; it was real. Beside him were James Worthy and Wilt Chamberlain, two other huge NBA stars. I nearly lost my mind. However, because I had been trained to control not only my muscles but also my emotions, I completed my routine as if nothing out of the ordinary had happened. I never did get to meet Magic, but James Worthy and Wilt Chamberlain came into the gym afterward to talk with us. Other NBA players from around the league had also come to the Wooden Center to work out during that time. We saw them on a regular basis, which was incredible for a basketball fan like me. However, in spite of the celebrity sightings, my adjustments to college life remained slow and miserable.

My teammates knew just how miserable and sad I was, and they tried everything they could do to help me. This included inviting me to go out with them to parties. Their hot spot was fraternity row, where they had wild parties with loud rock music (not my thing), and it seemed as if everyone was drunk out of his or her mind. They fell all over me, spilled their beer on me, and just laughed about it. "Du-u-de. Sorry." Back home, I went to parties where people drank, but they didn't get sloppy drunk. And they didn't play blaring rock music. They grooved to a unique blend of artists like Cameo, Doug E. Fresh, Run DMC, and Chuck

Brown, the Godfather of Go-Go. That said, at least the white frat parties weren't broken up by gunfire.

Sometimes back at home we'd be dancing or joking around when suddenly the crowd would start to disperse. We all knew what that meant: *someone* was about to get shot. "Let's go!" someone would say. If I didn't move fast enough, my friends pulled or nudged me along. We learned quickly that when someone said, "Go!" we had to do it quickly, no questions asked. Often, gunshots rang out before we managed to escape, turning our rapid walk into a sprint. There was no looking behind you to see what was going on because as we used to say, "Bullets have no name." We'd jump in the car, speed away, and find some other place to hang out—another party or a fast-food restaurant's parking lot. Parties back home were a lot different than UCLA's fraternity row.

I didn't want the beer and I didn't want the guns, but I did desire to socialize with other black students. Seeing that my lame attempts to reach out to peers outside of my athletic world were so unsuccessful, I just carried on with the people whose paths I crossed on a daily basis. I lived on the fourth floor of Sproul Hall. This is where I met another black student whose company I enjoyed. Tamyra was a pre-med student who hid the identity of her father because he was a professional athlete. She didn't want people to befriend her only because of his fame. She was determined not to live in his shadow and was ready to find her own way in the world. I liked that Tamyra was genuine and down to earth. We really hit it off. One thing we had in common was our desperation to socialize with other black students. So we set out on the quest together. Having Tamyra in my life was a Godsend. My days got better and my mood began to lift. Perhaps I'd make it after all.

Whether my mood was good or not, I still had to train daily. It was difficult, but as I began to see that I could be happy at UCLA, my attitude started to change. While I was practicing one day, one of my coaches, Ms. Val, told me I had the potential to win a national championship. I looked at her as if she were out of her mind. It still baffles me that I did not think I was any good even after accomplishing so much. Apart from my general sense of inferiority, another reason for my low self-esteem was the negative comments from my former coach, Mrs. Shaw, which still played over and over in my mind. "Kim Hamilton, you will never be as good as …! You don't have what it takes to …!" For all those years I strove to do my best, but deep inside, after hearing those words again and again, I stopped believing I truly could be the best. However, after that talk from Ms. Val, my attitude slowly began to change. Now I had the positive reinforcement I needed, and I started to train as if it were true.

January of 1987 came around, and it was time for our competition season to begin. My first meet at UCLA was nerve-wracking enough, but I had also been told that my favorite singer would be there to watch. Excited but a little nervous, I made my way through warm-ups. As warm-ups ended, I looked up and there she was. She was as beautiful as the pictures I had seen. Janet Jackson. As it turns out, I was only weeks away from performing her song "Control" in a dorm-wide lip-synching contest. So when I had a chance to meet her right before the competition started, I asked for some advice. In her sweet, shy voice with that gorgeous smile, she said, "Just have fun!" What a way to start the season!

Janet sat away from the general public so she would not be bothered as she watched the competition. We competed on vault first and then the uneven bars. When it came time to do the balance beam—my least favorite event—my nerves got the best of me. As I turned sideways on the beam to do a split jump, I found myself staring directly into Ms. Jackson's eyes. Ironically, this was the same spot in my routine when I had discovered Magic Johnson staring at me a few months earlier. But this time, instead of maintaining my composure, I fell off the beam. I was so embarrassed that I finished the rest of the competition totally deflated. The only good news was that it was my worst meet of the year. Things were about to go up from there.

Tamyra was my best friend outside of the gym, but Jill, another freshman, was my closest friend on the team. We, along with fellow freshman Shawn, were forced to carry the springboard when we traveled and do whatever else the upper classmen wanted us to do. Jill was my confidante, someone I could count on in my greatest time of need. We spent a lot of time cutting up together, doing funny things and causing a scene, whether it was singing in the gym or dancing in airports. Ms. Val called Jill and me "the twins," even though she was five-foot-two and Caucasian and I was five-foot-seven and African-American.

Jill and I always talked about how I would be in entertainment one day and she would be my lawyer. That actually happened some ten years later in 1996. I was visiting Jill in Chicago when I happened to mention that I was getting calls from friends around the country saying they saw my picture on billboards, in magazines, on airport dioramas, and in grocery stores. "Should I be concerned?" I asked.

"Yes, Kimmie, you should!" she retorted. That marked the beginning of our lawyer-client relationship, as she tried to find out why four major companies were using my picture to advertise their products. Jill proved to be as good a lawyer as she was a gymnast, and we were eventually able to settle out of court.

Another teammate I became close with during my freshman year was "Janey." She was a sophomore who had hosted me for my recruiting trip. If my financial state was at the low end of the spectrum, hers was at the total opposite end. She was a stylish dresser who frequented high-end department stores. Her dorm room bed was covered with satin sheets, and she drove a BMW.

In 1987 we had both started dating guys on UCLA's basketball team. On the night before home games, the basketball team would stay in the Bonaventure Hotel in downtown LA. One particular night, our boyfriends happened to be rooming together, so they asked us to come down and visit them. We weren't sure we should go because they were under curfew, but they told us they could easily sneak us into their room.

When we arrived at the hotel, we were like ninjas, peeking around corners and hiding so that no one would see us. We didn't want to get caught by a coach, but we also didn't want any of the other players to see us. We were "good girls," and we didn't want anyone to think more of our little visit than it was. When we finally found their room, our hearts were racing. We made it! We hung out with the guys for about an hour, talking and watching TV. Then we made our secret trek back out again.

Afterward, we spent a few hours touring high-rise condos along Wilshire Boulevard. We pretended to be students from wealthy families who were looking for a place to buy. Come to think of it, I was doing a lot more pretending than Janey was.

The entire gymnastics team treated me like a little sister. They encouraged me and made sure I had everything I needed. Though I felt like an outsider in so many ways, they refused to let me isolate myself. They went out of their way to make sure I knew they cared. I could not have remained at UCLA without them.

By the middle of my freshman year, I was feeling more at home than ever. There was now more laughter than tears, and I was actually enjoying my experience. Another friend I had outside of the gym was a young man named Vaughn. He was an African-American freshman as well. I got to know him because his room was right across from the girls' bathroom on my floor. He, in fact, showed me how to wash clothes. (I never had to do that sort of thing at home because I was always at the gym.) Vaughn's parents were well off, and he planned on becoming a lawyer. Where I grew up, it was almost wrong to have lofty goals like that. If you did, you were accused of either trying to be white or thinking you were better than the rest. Either way, it seemed wrong to want a better life. But in Vaughn's world, his goals were both admirable and attainable.

It was during a conversation with Vaughn that I developed a sense of shame about who I was and where I came from. I had become so comfortable around him that I began to talk freely about the things I did back in Virginia. At one point in our conversation I think I mentioned the incident about my friend picking me up and seeing my dad and his cousin with a huge pile of weed on the table. Back home, people laughed when I told that story, so I expected the same type of response from Vaughn. Instead, he looked at me with a concerned look of disbelief and said, "What?" Immediately, I knew I had shared too much. "That's never happened to you before?" I asked, breaking the awkward silence with a shy smile.

"No!" he exclaimed. He had no idea what I was talking about. At that moment, I realized I didn't even fit in with the other African-Americans at school. I had been self-conscious about my background with my gymnastics friends, but I assumed that he would be able to relate to my experiences. It was obvious I had painted my fellow African-American students with too broad of a brush. Before that incident, I thought the way I grew up was normal. Now I felt there was no place for me to be myself.

This discovery led me to retreat again toward isolation. Coupled with my shyness, this didn't do much for my reputation. Things reached a point where I was so focused on gymnastics and what I would have to do in practice that day that someone could literally walk within a foot of me and I would not even notice. If I wasn't thinking about training, my mind was on issues at home—my mother's safety or my financial situation. My mind was always struggling with one kind of burden or another. There was no one else I could talk to but God. I sure hoped *he* wasn't appalled by my experiences.

Some people interpreted my aloofness as being stuck up or snobbish. Word got back to me that other African-American students called me "Whitewash" behind my back because I was the only black gymnast on the university team. They said I only socialized with white students and that I thought I was too good for them. I shrugged it off, but it hurt because people were judging me, even though they didn't know anything about me apart from what they read in the press. Little did they realize, I was the complete opposite of what they thought. I didn't think I was too good; I thought I wasn't good enough. I didn't think they would accept me because unlike many of their parents, who went to college before them, my momma had only gotten her high school diploma, and my daddy only had a ninth grade education. When they were visiting their fathers at work, I was visiting mine in jail. When they were driving their cars to school, I was taking the bus. When they were getting money from the ATM machine, I was being rejected because I didn't even have the twenty-dollar minimum balance that was needed to get money from my bank account.

All my life I had been surrounded by financial struggles. When I was a kid, they were always Momma's struggles. But now they were my struggles too. Seeing as I couldn't afford textbooks, I would check them out from the library when they were available, borrow from a classmate, or simply do without. I didn't think I could go to my coaches because Jerry had already told me that I'd have to take care of books on my own. My grades suffered as a result, but I was able to keep my GPA above a 2.0, so I remained eligible to compete.

One day I was sitting in the weight room, crying about my situation, when a young man asked what was wrong. I told him I was struggling in school because I couldn't afford textbooks. On the spot, he gave me a one hundred-dollar bill. I was speechless. I had never even seen a one hundred-dollar bill before, much less had someone give me one. I couldn't believe someone I didn't know very well would just help me out like that. He said I didn't have to worry about paying him back, but I couldn't agree to that. In my mind that was too much money for someone to just give away. It took several months, but somehow Momma scraped up enough money to repay him.

Before that moment, I thought I was all alone. But that act of kindness inspired me to keep going. Perhaps I wasn't so alone after all. There it was again—another answer to prayer. Just when I thought God wasn't there for me, he did more than I even thought to ask.

Ultimately, my understanding of our financial situation would culminate during my first year sociology class. We were studying socioeconomic status. I knew what Momma made, so I ran my finger down the list of salaries in my textbook that were categorized into upper-middle class, lower-middle class, etc. I had to go a long way down the chart before I found Momma's salary range. The textbook used only four letters to describe such a person: P-O-O-R. *My goodness,* I thought, *we are poor.* You would think I should have known that already, but it was the first time it really hit me. For the remainder of class, all I could think was that I had to warn my mother about our precarious state of being. *Surely she is in the dark about this,* I thought. How would she respond to the news?

When class ended, I ran to a payphone and called Momma. When she answered, I took a deep breath and said, "Momma, did you know that we're poor?" She replied in her soft, reassuring voice. "Yeah, baby, I know we're poor."

All sorts of thoughts tumbled through my mind at that point. *Why didn't she ever tell me that before? Maybe it is because I never asked.* Our needs were met, and that's all that mattered. I guess I didn't realize the extent of our financial situation because to me, people who were poor lived on the streets. They didn't have jobs or food to eat. We had all of those things. Yes, we didn't always have our *own* place, but we always had some kind of roof over our heads. The sacrifices my parents made to keep me clothed and fed gave me a sense of privilege, not poverty. I thought our financial struggles were the result of expensive gymnastics training, not lack of income.

Now it became even more important for me to take advantage of the opportunity to attend this prestigious university. I knew it would be my only chance to achieve a higher education and to possibly break the cycle of poverty in which my family had been trapped. I was determined to do well not only in gymnastics but also in academics. An apparent curse of discovering my family's lack had suddenly been transformed into a blessing that would drive me to persevere.

FOURTEEN

# MY "BORROWED" FAMILY

During my freshman year, Jerry kept saying he wanted me to meet a woman named Jackie. He said I reminded him of her, and he felt she would be a real encouragement to me. I had no idea who he was talking about, but I trusted his judgment.

Then one day we were walking beside Pauley Pavilion when this tall, muscular African-American woman approached from the opposite direction. "Jackie!" Jerry called out. She stopped to chat, and Jerry introduced her to me as Jackie Joyner-Kersee. That's right, the same woman who would win three gold, one silver, and two bronze Olympic medals and become the world record holder for the heptathlon. She greeted me with a warm smile that immediately set me at ease. It may have been that Jerry had already briefed her about me because even with his short introduction of who I was, I felt that she understood me and actually cared about how I was doing. From that point on she took me under her wing and became like the big sister I never had. Jackie and her husband, Bobby Kersee, who coached not only Jackie but

173

also Florence Griffith (Joyner), Valerie Brisco-Hooks, and Gail Devers, were like my family away from home.

Jackie came from a rough neighborhood in St. Louis, so she could relate to the cultural differences I was enduring at UCLA as well as the challenges of being a student athlete. Having lost her mother, she was no stranger to pain. Sure, her pain was quite different than what I had experienced, but I believe this gave her a sensitivity that others didn't have. Jackie invited me into her home, where we talked about school, dreams, the "what not to dos" and the "who not to do it withs." She marveled about the crazy skills gymnasts had to perform, from double back flips and tumbling across a four inch wide "stick," to wearing leotards that rose up too high and having to leave it there while you competed. I, in turn, marveled about her many events in track and field, throwing "spears" (javelin) and "iron balls" (shot put) and especially having to run long distances in the hot sun and land in the dirt after a long jump. "It's not dirt," she corrected me. "It's sand." We continued to compare stories, eventually concluding that we should each stick with our respective sports.

Jackie and Bobby were so funny together. They always gave each other a hard time. Bobby would tell stories about how Jackie complained during practices. Jackie would respond with, "Puhlease!" Then she'd go on to explain how mean he was to her during her demanding workouts. They would playfully argue about who had gotten the story right. Despite the digs, their coach-athlete relationship on the track seemed to work just as well as their husband-wife relationship at home.

My biggest question to Jackie about being married to her coach was, "Since you spend so much time together, how do you handle him knowing about everything you eat?" That's probably a question only a gymnast can understand. For me, that was enough to be a deal breaker. She looked around to make sure he wasn't listening then gave me a sly smile and assured me that Bobby didn't see *everything* she ate.

Jackie and Bobby continually checked in on me, and I cried on Jackie's shoulder on numerous occasions. There was one specific time when Momma called to tell me that she had arrived home from work and discovered that Daddy had thrown all of her belongings onto the street. She had no choice but to move back in with Grandma Justine. Jackie was the first and only person I told about the situation. As usual, even though she couldn't do anything about it, she gave me encouragement and comfort. She would tell me that I could make it no matter what was going on at home, and she persuaded me to focus on what I needed to get done in the gym and in class. "It's gon' be all right," she would say. From Jackie, I learned how special it was that I was a black gymnast and how I could use my platform to have a positive influence on others. I also learned a lot about living life with class and dignity. If I wasn't learning something from what she told me face-to-face, I learned it from watching the way she carried herself. Above all, Jackie taught me that no matter how successful you become, you can still remain grounded and have a positive impact on those around you.

Speaking of positive impacts, during that time, *The Cosby Show* was my favorite television show. It was the first time I had ever seen a successful black family with a positive father figure on TV. Bill Cosby was the type of dad I wished I had. One of the perks of going to UCLA was the opportunity to meet the celebrities who used the campus facilities to stay in shape. Bill Cosby was one of them. On my way to class I often saw him jogging around the track in Drake Stadium. One day I worked up the courage to go out and meet him.

I timed it perfectly so I could join him when he came around the turn. It was quite obvious that I didn't just happen to be there jogging around the track in jeans and my favorite pair of wrestling shoes, but I ran up beside him and said, "Hi, Mr. Cosby." He greeted me with a jovial hello and asked if I liked to jog. I could have said yes just to impress him. Instead, I told him I didn't like jogging at all and that I was just out there to meet him. Looking back on the experience, I probably could have been a little less direct. But he just laughed it off and chided me about how bad it was for me to jog in my wrestling shoes. He couldn't help but be a father.

As we jogged, we talked a little about the show. I told him that I didn't have a TV in my dorm room but my momma was taping the shows on the VCR back home so I could watch them during the summer. He said it was good that I didn't have a TV and that I should be studying anyway. He reminded me of the importance of a good education and encouraged me to get at least a 2.7 grade point average. At the time, my GPA was nowhere near a 2.7, despite the fact that I had graduated high school as the salutatorian. My inability to afford books was taking a toll on my grades. Books or not, you'd better believe that after Bill Cosby told me to study hard, my study habits changed immediately.

After that first meeting, Mr. Cosby and I ran into each other quite often. He even gave me a nickname, "Funny Pants," because of the pants I was wearing when we first met. The conversations almost always had to do with how I was doing academically. He helped me to understand the importance of my being at UCLA and that I needed to take full advantage of the position I was in. His stressing the fact that my academics needed to be taken seriously was a huge motivation. I was used to having someone to talk to about my athletic goals, but this was the first person outside a guidance counselor who ever expressed such an interest in my academics and helped me to set goals in that area as well. Here I was, thousands of miles from home, getting fatherly advice from America's favorite father. I would love to think that my encounter with Mr. Cosby was a unique experience, but I'm positive that meeting him is a life-defining moment for just about everyone and that they walk away from that encounter a better person. I know I certainly did.

As I look back on my experiences with Mr. Cosby, Jackie, and others, I can see that once again God was looking out for me by putting people in my life, who encouraged me right when I needed it.

# FIFTEEN

# A GIRL HAS GOT TO EAT!

Just about all of the female students talked about the freshman fifteen, which is how many pounds a typical college student gained during his or her freshman year. Unlike the regular student population, the gymnasts had to weigh in regularly. Our coaches and support team kept a close eye on every ounce, which was quite easy considering the tightly fitted leotards we were required to wear. There was a lot of pressure for us to weigh in light and to look lean and tight.

I had a difficult time keeping my weight down because I wasn't eating properly. At home I never went hungry, but there were times when the refrigerator was bare and we had to be creative with what we had. In a sense, my mind was trained to be thankful for my daily bread because I never knew what tomorrow would bring. It could be only a bowl of broccoli, some hot dogs and beans, or potted meat and crackers. On a good night it would be spaghetti topped with a sauce that Momma made from ketchup and a few seasonings.

Life in the dorms was a different story. Breakfast, lunch, and dinner were served every day, and it was always "all you can eat." So my "don't know what tomorrow may bring" mentality quickly went out the window. Watching me load up at that buffet would have put a three hundred-pound offensive lineman to shame. I was so excited about the quantity and variety of food choices that I made multiple trips to the buffet so I could try a bit of everything. I *loved* bread and cheese, so anything Italian was my favorite. Spaghetti, lasagna, pizza, and rolls, yes, hot buttered rolls, were my weakness. Of course, I always cleaned my plate—or shall I say, plates—because wasting food was not an option where I came from. (I still have issues with that thought pattern today, some twenty years later.) I have embarrassed myself many times by making too many trips to the buffet. I usually don't realize that I am out of control until someone points it out. Now, in some instances, I will eat a full meal before I go to a function so I won't embarrass myself. It still amazes me how the things from our childhood affect us into adulthood.

Seeing that I was struggling with my weight, one of my coaches said that the simplest way to lose weight was to stop eating. I was eager to see results, so I often skipped meals, but this only caused me to binge the next time I ate. This cycle played out for a few weeks until I concluded it was hopeless. Starving myself was never going to work because I loved food way too much. In fact, I secretly longed to become a food critic so I could travel the world, enjoying the best foods available. Therefore, I decided to try a difference tactic for weight loss.

For breakfast and lunch I drank a can of tomato juice or mango nectar. I took slow sips and swished the juice around in my mouth before swallowing, hoping I could trick my body into thinking it was solid food. But when I passed by the food court on the way back from class, the smell of pizza and hamburgers drew me in. They had healthy options as well, but I had only a few quarters to my name, so I could only afford to buy junk food like apple fritters, which I did often.

Another weight-loss tactic I observed my teammates using was throwing up after a meal. It seemed to be working for them, so I decided to give it a try. It didn't last long, though, because I thought throwing up was just plain nasty. It tasted a lot better going down than it did coming up. I'm glad it grossed me out so much because it really could have become a problem for me, as it was for some other gymnasts I knew.

My next attempt at shedding the pounds was intense exercise. In the wee hours of the morning, I ran the Drake Stadium stairs, hoping to slim up my thighs. I forced myself up and down the stairs until I screamed because of my burning leg muscles. Tears ran down my cheeks as anger and disappointment filled my mind. I felt that I was fighting a battle I could never win.

In the long run, the methods I used to lose weight during that time probably did more harm than good, and I don't recommend them to anyone. But back then, I didn't understand what good nutrition was all about. Fortunately, the team brought in a nutritionist who taught us healthier and more practical ways to combine exercise and diet. I learned the importance of staying away from high fat foods and sugars and drinking lots of water. It sounded like a great plan, but it wasn't easy to follow because I had already created so many bad habits. Knowing I needed to stay away from certain types of foods made me want them even more. Plus, the taste of good food brought me so much comfort when I was down.

I don't know if I ever turned my eating habits around completely, but I did cut down on the pizzas, Tommy Burgers, and apple fritters that had become a mainstay in my diet. This gave me some control over my weight, but it still remained a stressor in my life. My heart goes out to those who struggle with anorexia, bulimia, and obsessive exercise because I understand how someone can reach a point of believing there is no other way. Before I went to college I saw the deadly effects these diseases had on other gymnasts. Now I was tempted to fall into that same trap. Ultimately, people are drawn to such things because of a desperate desire for acceptance or to meet a certain standard. Still, I know there is hope in every situation, a hope that I found only months after struggling with the problem on my own.

# SIXTEEN

# HARD WORK PAYS OFF

As the year progressed, my routines improved and became more consistent. When I competed on the national team, I had to perform both compulsory and optional routines, two different routines on each of four events. In college, we were only required to do optional routines. Therefore, I had more time to focus on the skills that gave me problems. My coaches helped me execute my skills to the fullest, so I excelled in ways I never dreamed possible. In addition, all the fun we had during workouts helped me enjoy training much more than I had back at home. As a result, I worked even harder.

Back in Richmond I faced a taxing workout with high repetitions. We were to be working at *all* times. If you were resting between routines, your rest consisted of V-ups, push-ups, or drills. Standing still was a no-no. We got in trouble and were relegated to even *more* work if we even had the appearance of slacking off. Unless we were severely injured, meaning you had to go to the emergency room in the back of an ambulance, we still had to work out. You may have had to walk with a limp, but you'd better do a no-fall beam routine without whining and still stick the dismount. We were trained to be tough.

At UCLA, however, we could sing, dance, and play around as long as we completed our assignments. There was lots of laughter from the coaches and the gymnasts. We were free to express our personalities. If we got injured, there were trainers there to take care of us, and rest was not forbidden. The coaches knew that we were all *extremely* driven and had come from disciplined backgrounds. So they trusted us when we said we were injured or needed to take a break. Sometimes they even had to stop *us* from pushing ourselves too hard. The work ethics instilled in us by our club coaches made it possible for this type of environment to exist while still giving us an incredible amount of success. We competed each week, and in each meet I accomplished a new goal. This helped me move forward and peak at the right time of the season.

I was also encouraged by my excellent teammates. Some were former national team members like me, one was a Canadian Olympian, and others were event specialists. Their talent encouraged me to live up to the positive reputation this team had as great athletes. I was in a constant competition with myself. If I had a break in my routine, the next time I performed it, my goal would be for that break to disappear. I wanted to be as good as my teammates because I knew that the better we were individually, the better we were as a team.

As a result of our efforts, that first year our team made it to the NCAA National Gymnastics Championships, which were held in Salt Lake City. I was to compete in the all-around competition, which meant that I had to do exceptionally well on each event.

Something very special happened when I performed my floor routine during the preliminary round. My dance coach, Ms. Val, had created a routine that took into account my love of performing. She choreographed unique dance moves that caught the judges and spectators off guard. It was as much fun to perform as it was to watch. On this particular day, I felt as if I was at one with the sold-out arena of spectators. As I moved through my routine, I looked directly into the eyes of various people and flashed a smile, smirked, or winked. These strangers became my friends, as I performed not an ordinary floor routine but in my mind a stage play that was comedic, dramatic, and full of suspense.

When the music ended, I held my final pose longer than usual, as if it were an exclamation point to one of the best routines I had ever executed. Finally, I stood up, signaled the judges that I was finished, and then ran toward my teammates and coaches. They embraced me and exclaimed how excited they were with my performance. I was happy, exhausted, and relieved to have made it through the first round.

As I bent over to catch my breath, I felt a tap on my shoulder. "Kimmie, look!" I stood up and saw thousands of spectators rise to their feet and applaud—for me! Jerry told me to go back out to greet them. I ran to the middle of the floor and hesitantly saluted the sold-out crowd. I couldn't stop a huge smile from spreading across my face as I waved and sheepishly mouthed the words *thank you*.

As I scanned the crowd, I spotted Momma and Daddy. They had scrounged up just enough money to make the trip. Even though they were separated, they flew in together and shared the same hotel room. They could have watched the competition on television, but there was nothing like being there in person. They followed my every move and offered their support from a distance whenever I glanced their way. Tears filled my eyes as I remembered all my parents had sacrificed to help me reach this moment. Now gymnastics fans from all over the country were giving a standing ovation for UCLA's first black female gymnast—their own flesh and blood.

At the same time, having both of my parents at the competition was difficult for me. My mother was still on the receiving end of Daddy's complaints and anger. When we were all together, Momma and I walked on eggshells, still trying to keep the peace. I saw the sadness in her eyes as she struggled to be perfect so he would not be disappointed. But even our best efforts failed. I always walked away from our times together angry and saddened. But as I relished this moment of accomplishment, I could only see the positive in having them both there to celebrate with me. I was overwhelmed with emotion as the cheers and applause went on and on. Never had I experienced so much satisfaction as an athlete. *Thank you, God!* The value and love that I had always craved was now coming from perfect strangers. To keep it coming, all I had to do was perform well. *The pressure was on.*

My performance in the preliminaries earned me a spot in the finals for two events, one of which was the floor exercise. On floor, my toughest competition was

Kelly Garrison. She had competed with me on the US National Team and went on to compete in the 1988 Olympics. She did an amazing routine with skills that were of the highest difficulty. Even watching her warm up was intimidating. It was hard for me to hold on to my coach's belief that I could become a national champion. All of my old feelings of insecurity came flooding back. After I warmed up, I went off to the side to get some last-minute tips from my coaches. Some of the advice was technical, but the most helpful was the encouragement to "just have fun."

As my turn drew closer, my heart pounded as if it were going to leap out of my chest. I could hear each beat in my ears. Panic washed over me. Suddenly, I wanted to die. When I finally stepped up to the sideline and waited to salute the judges, I asked myself why I continued to put myself through this. I vowed that this would be my last competition. When I was finished, I would quit the sport once and for all. I hated the feeling of fear, panic, and the newfound pressure to please this wonderful audience. Suddenly, the head judge's flag went up, signaling it was okay for me to proceed. I raised my right hand, flashed a fake smile, and then got into character. Immediately, I felt the panic recede. Let the fun begin.

All I needed was a clean routine with no falls, and the national title would be within my grasp. At the time, though, I wasn't thinking about winning, just surviving and staying on my feet until the end. The music that accompanied my routine was a combination of the themes from *The Twilight Zone* and *Friday the 13th*, an odd medley, but it created a foundation for an interesting display of skill and emotion. Once again, I got caught up in the performance and had the time of my life.

After my second tumbling pass, though, my body was exhausted. The high altitude in Utah was not my friend. My lungs burned with each breath. My legs and arms felt as if they had twenty-pound weights tied to them. I still had a long dance series and the last tumbling pass to go. I labored through my dance, trying my best to make it look effortless. Then I worked my way into the corner and prepared for my final tumbling pass. I took two deep burning breaths and forced my body to run as fast as it could. It felt as though I was running through waist-deep water. But I muscled up enough speed to complete my pass and stick the landing. One last leap and down I went into my final pose. I signaled the judges that I was finished then exited the floor.

For a second time, the audience rose to its feet and cheered. Again, my coaches pushed me back out onto the floor to greet the crowd. One by one, the judges flashed their scores. A roar of excitement greeted each one. The final score, a meet record of 9.80, launched me into the number one spot. I became the first UCLA woman to win an individual NCAA gymnastics title. When the news was announced, the crowd rose to its feet, yet again in wild applause. I couldn't believe I was the winner. I'd come a long way from that first day I set foot on campus.

I ran onto the floor, waved to the crowd, congratulated the others, and then took my spot atop the podium. After the awards were handed out, we raised our trophies above our heads. Ms. Val knew it even before the season began. Now I knew it too. I was the 1987 NCAA National Floor Exercise Champion!

# SEVENTEEN

# HOME SWEET HOME?

By the end of my first year, I had won my first national title and was an All-American. When I first arrived on campus, I never dreamed of all the wonderful things I would experience. When summer came, though, I couldn't wait to get home. I was homesick and anxious to see Momma, my friends, and the whole season of *The Cosby Show* waiting for me on VHS.

As I saw the beautiful green trees on our descent into Dulles Airport, I was struck by how different it was from the concrete buildings and roadways I had seen when I first landed in LA. It gave me a new appreciation for my home state of Virginia. Momma met me at the airport. Then we drove two hours back to Richmond, during which she caught me up on all the latest happenings.

During the drive, I looked at Momma for what seemed like the first time. I realized I had avoided looking at her during high school, perhaps because I didn't want to see a reflection of my future self. But now I saw her differently. I had such an appreciation for her character and the sacrifices she made for me. That summer would mark the beginning of a major shift in our relationship. I went from wanting to avoid being seen with her to walking through the mall hand in hand with her. I realized I absolutely adored this woman.

As we exited the highway in Richmond, it felt so good to be home. The neighborhood was the same as I had left it. We rode down Cary Street past the gas station, the liquor store, and the run-down row houses. A woman walked up the street with her hair in bright pink rollers and dirty fluffy slippers on her feet, even though it was in the middle of the afternoon. A man who looked as if he had worn the same clothes for weeks stood on the corner counting his change while sipping out of a bottle wrapped in a brown paper bag. That's right; nothing had changed.

The next block was Grandma Justine's house. There was the same brick sidewalk and the concrete stairs to welcome me. The first thing I did when I walked through the door was hug and kiss Grandma Justine. I also greeted my cousin who still lived with her. Momma was living there too, seeing as she and Daddy had failed to reconcile after he put her out of the apartment. In a way, you could say circumstances forced Momma and me to draw closer that summer. We had to sleep in the same bed.

I planned to return to school lean and mean, so I ate as little as possible while at home, just enough to keep me from passing out. I couldn't get away with doing that during gymnastics season because I wouldn't have enough energy to make it through our workouts. I slept as much as I could so I could save energy. Then I'd use what little energy I had to work at a video rental store and work out at the gym. I trained like crazy on the stair climber and lifted weights. By the end of the summer I was able to shed ten pounds, but they proved difficult to keep off.

Not long after I returned home, I got a call from a show called the *Ebony Jet Showcase*. It was the only national TV show at the time that focused on the black community. I had been featured in *Ebony* magazine during the school year. They had been following my career and wanted to come to my house and do an interview. I fell silent as I looked around Grandma Justine's kitchen and thought about how the other rooms in the house looked. Even though it was *always* tidy, the furniture was excessively worn. There were dirty walls from the constant hand traffic of the grandkids, and the hall floors were covered with several different patterns of linoleum, which had been *nailed* down instead of glued. I had been embarrassed when my classmates made fun of where I lived when I was in the sixth grade. There was no way I was about to let the whole world do the same. I asked the show's producer if we could do the interview in a nearby park instead. He agreed, but in the end, the interview did not take place. Others would have been disappointed, but all I felt was relief. I could still keep my home life a secret from my UCLA peers.

I spent most of my nights that summer watching episodes of *The Cosby Show*. I also watched free videos that I was allowed to bring home from work. Many of the videos I chose were about death and violence. I was still fixated with death and the gory scenes that portrayed it. It was probably a good reflection of my inner thoughts at the time. I did not value life, not even my own. I saw no real reason for my existence, and death was just another thing. Although I had been successful in my gymnastics career, I still had deep scars from my relationship with my father, and that anger continued to manifest itself in violent thoughts.

My anger toward my father was so great that Momma had to force me to visit him while I was home. I didn't want to see him because I resented him, and I knew that any time the two of them were in the same room he would say something to Momma that made her feel ashamed. Every time this happened it was like a dagger in my heart too.

During a visit with Daddy that summer, we were laughing, talking, and getting along just fine. Then the topic got around to me having my wisdom teeth removed, which had happened a little less than two years earlier. Suddenly, his anger kindled. "What?" he exclaimed. "You got your wisdom teeth out? Y'all don't tell me nothin'!"

My heart sank. Of all the moments I had spent with him over the past few years, that time was my most precious. He took me to the dentist to have the surgery and stayed home for two days to take care of me afterward. He fed me, helped me clean my wounds, and even held me in his arms while I cried from the pain. And now, fewer than two years later, he didn't remember a thing about it. That precious time had been the one thing that I held on to as proof that he loved me. Now even that was shattered. My anger and sadness grew exponentially after that visit. I was tired of hoping and searching for a light at the end of the tunnel of our relationship. I had done my duty. I visited him that one time and did not go back again that summer.

---

One night I decided to forego the videos and spend some time with my friends. I informed the guys, who usually had marijuana, that UCLA had mandatory random drug testing for all of their athletes, so I could not be around weed anymore. Secretly, I was glad about this fact because it gave me an excuse not to participate. Even though my friends had never coerced me to smoke, I was such a people pleaser that I would do just about anything to fit in. The guys responded greatly; they respected my boundaries and even tried to shelter me from exposure to secondhand smoke. As the night wore on, we got hungry and headed for a teen hangout that was still open. Robin parked her car, and then we met up with the others in the parking lot.

Robin and I were walking ahead of the guys, when I noticed a couple of young men leaning against a car. I vaguely heard one of them say something to us, but I didn't quite make it out. I glanced at them and nodded but didn't stop. That was an automatic response. I was taught you greeted the people you walked by whether they looked like an upstanding citizen, a hardcore criminal, or a drunk staggering down the street. It was respectful and usually helped you avoid needless confrontation. In that split second I noted that the young black men looked quite normal. They were well dressed, and there was nothing unusual about them.

Evidently, though, my guy friends didn't like what the other guys had said. They exchanged words, and I thought that was the end of it. But as I reached the door to the restaurant, I heard one of the young men yell in a loud and forceful voice. I turned around to see what was happening and found myself staring down the barrel of a revolver. I had been watching glamorized scenes of artificial death on TV all summer. Now the very real possibility of death was staring me in the face, and there was nothing glamorous about it at all.

My gaze shifted from the gun to the eyes of this angry young man and then back to the gun again. My first thought was to take the gun away like Daddy had taught me when I was in middle school. Did he know that such a day would come, or was such an event just an inevitable part of daily life for him? Either way, I realized my friends would be at risk of getting shot if I tried to twist the gun out of his hand. So I just stood there with a disgusted smirk on my face. I had way too much attitude to be scared.

In that brief moment I don't remember seeing my life flash before my eyes. Instead, I saw all of my failed attempts at finding personal significance. Ever since I could remember, I had longed to be loved and accepted, especially by my father. I wanted to be my father's little princess. I also wanted others to like me. But none of my attempts to win approval, not even my significant athletic accomplishments, had worked. Now I stood there helpless, my fate in the hands of this young man. No longer did it matter how I grew up or whether my father was in my life. It didn't matter what people thought about me or that I had just won my first NCAA championship title. Everything I thought would give me a sense of value suddenly meant absolutely nothing.

A moment later he swung the gun away from me and pointed it at someone else. Then he moved down the line, threatening each one of my friends in turn. With a flick of my hand, I walked past him toward the rear of the restaurant. Only then did the fear hit me. I suddenly realized that my display of indifference could very well have made him even angrier and that it was highly possible I would feel a bullet pierce my back at any moment. I kept walking and braced myself for the pain that I was sure would come. But it never did.

When I got around behind the restaurant and out of harm's way, my muscles went limp, and I fell to my knees. I waited for the sound of a gunshot. "God, please don't let him kill my friends!" I prayed, as if I thought God were real. Truthfully, I wasn't sure. I had been afraid that if I truly believed in God he would disappoint me just like Daddy had. Maybe he would show up sometimes but disappear when I needed him most. I also worried that I could never live up to his expectations. Or worse, that I'd place my belief in him, as I did with Santa Claus when I was little, only to find out that he wasn't real. Even though I wasn't sure about God's existence, there was no one else for me to call upon at that moment. So I did what I always heard my mother doing: I prayed.

My heart beat out of control, and it was hard for me to catch my breath. But I finally gathered enough strength to stand up and peer around the corner. Then I heard Robin cry out, and my fears for my own safety disappeared. I ran back and found her on the ground as the guys gathered around to comfort her. I thought the gunman had harmed her, but they told me she was just afraid. The young man and his friends were gone. We all walked away from the situation unharmed, but I couldn't help thinking there had to be more to life. You live, you die, and for what? That question was still unresolved as I headed back to UCLA that fall.

# EIGHTEEN

# FINALLY, SOME ANSWERS!

I returned to UCLA feeling a lot more comfortable than that first day of my freshman year. Over the summer, I had even saved up enough money to buy some of my textbooks.

Things weren't completely rosy, though. The relationship I had with the basketball player during the latter part of my freshman year came to an abrupt halt when I realized it was one big lie. During the first quarter of school, I went to his place after my workout and found him in his room with a young woman. He acted as if he barely knew me when, for months, he had made it *clear* that he and I had an exclusive relationship. To put the icing on this tasteless cake, she sat there, nicely dressed, and looked at me as I stood there in my UCLA baggy sweats with a huge stinky gym bag draped across my body and said, "Oh! You're the little gymnast." I looked at him, waiting for him to tell her I was *also* his little girlfriend, and he said *nothing*. Needless to say, I went "off" on him, and that was the end of the relationship. This wreaked havoc on my emotions. Having a steady boyfriend was one way I attempted to get the love I craved. Ending the relationship meant that I was alone again, not to mention embarrassed that everyone knew he was playing me but *me*.

After the breakup, I often cried during practice and had to go to the restroom to pull myself together. When I stayed in there too long, Ms. Val came in and gave me a pep talk. One thing I remember her saying was that it was *his* loss, not mine. I looked up at her with surprise. "Yes, it is *his* loss, not yours," she repeated. She knew firsthand what a *bad* guy he was. I won't get into how, but trust me, she knew. And with these simple words, I was on my way to recovery.

I didn't get asked out very often back then, and when I did, it was usually by other athletes. But my experience with the basketball player had soured me on the idea, so I refused to date anyone involved in athletics. After a while, I got tired of waiting for a "normal guy" (meaning a non-athlete) to ask me out, so I decided to relinquish my ban.

Around that time someone introduced me to a young man named Corwin Anthony, who was a football player. I could tell right away that he was different from the other jocks I'd met. He wasn't arrogant and full of himself. He seemed humble and very respectful. He didn't pressure me physically and expect anything from me, like others had done. I had to literally fight a couple of his teammates off me on previous occasions when our seemingly innocent conversations ended up with them trying to take advantage of me. I must have been really naïve because I never saw it coming. Corwin took things slowly and carefully, as if I were a delicate flower who needed to be handled with care. I didn't know what made him that way, but I knew I liked it.

One Sunday afternoon I was at his apartment when I saw a Bible on his desk. I asked him about it, and he told me he had taken it to church that morning. Immediately, I assumed he was lying. I had never known any young man, much less a football player, who was interested in God. I decided to lay a little trap by asking him what he had learned at church that day. To my surprise, he opened up his Bible and proceeded to tell me, verse by verse, what the sermon was about. It was so strange, but it also felt so good.

I rarely went to church after I started doing gymnastics because my meets usually took place on weekends, but I did have a thirst to know God. I often pulled out the Bible my aunt Ruth and uncle Vernon gave me when I was feeling sad, which was often, but I had a difficult time understanding what it meant.

Corwin, on the other hand, came from a family deeply devoted to their faith. His grandfather was the founding pastor of their church in Bakersfield, California; his father was a deacon, and several of his fourteen aunts and uncles were pastors, deacons, and active as well. He was brought up in the church, and it had a heavy influence on his life. So going to church on a Sunday and actually remembering what the pastor said was normal for him.

As I got to know Corwin better, I found myself wanting whatever it was that gave him so much peace and made him such a caring guy. A few weeks later he told me something that changed my life. First, he shared how much God loved me, and that before I was even born he had a plan for my life. It was the first time I had ever heard such a thing. Although Momma and Grandma Justine were Christians and talked about God, they had never explained how to have my own relationship with him.

He went on to tell me that all of us are flawed by sin (or wrongdoing) and can never attain perfection through our own efforts. As a gymnast who strove for perfection daily but never attained it, I could relate with that. But then he said that as a result, we were destined to death, spiritual separation from God. I didn't think it sounded fair that our inability to be perfect human beings would lead us to death. I could understand receiving a low score, but don't I get something for my efforts? He told me that it's not about *our* efforts, and because God knows that we are incapable of perfection in and of ourselves, he provided a way to break free from sin and its consequences when he came down to earth as Jesus and "took the hit" that was meant for us. He provided a way out of death and all of the pain we go through as a result of our bad choices and hurtful attitudes. Jesus suffered for us so we could live in relationship with God. Corwin taught me that God is the one who gives us the power to change our desires and to act on what is good and true. He could help me change too, if I let him.

As I heard those words, I realized this was exactly what I had been searching for. For so long I had worked to make my life better. As an athlete, I'd been taught that if you set your goals and worked hard, you could reach them. Yet in my personal life all of my efforts to attain my goals of happiness and peace resulted only in temporary satisfaction. I thought if I could excel in athletics it would bring contentment or if I gained the approval and love of others it would give me a sense of value. But the results of my efforts proved to be fleeting and were always followed by the same old pain, emptiness, and the nagging feeling that there had to be more.

Corwin said I could change all of that, if I wanted. Then he helped me pray a simple and honest prayer asking God to forgive me for all the things I had done wrong. I asked him to guide my life and help me to live out his plans for me. I can't say I felt anything extraordinarily different afterward, but I knew in my heart that something significant had happened. The God I had cried out to when my parents were fighting, when I was struggling to perform a routine, and on the night my friends and I were held at gunpoint, wasn't imaginary like Santa Claus. He was real.

I wish I could tell you my life was easier after that, but it took a lot of time for God to expose the lies I believed about him and myself, and it took a lot of persuading before I was willing to embrace the truths that would set me free. But at least the process had begun. I began to live my life in a way that honored God, others, and myself. My do-or-die approach to my gymnastics turned into a healthy desire to please God in everything I did. I stopped being so hard on myself when I wasn't perfect but still maintained the drive to be the best athlete I could be. My language also changed.

Expletives were removed from my vocabulary, and my approach toward others became more caring, forgiving, and gentle.

I was beginning to learn that as shameful and destructive as my behavior could be, God loved me unconditionally, and he was always willing to gather me back into his arms and forgive me. Best of all, he never stopped believing in me. He also gave me wisdom so I could clean up the messes I made and get on with living the life he created me to live.

As my relationship with God began to blossom, I also grew closer to Corwin, to the point where we became sexually intimate. To me, it was a natural progression in any dating relationship. But then one day Corwin sat up in bed and said, "I want to stop."

"Stop what?" I asked.

"Stop doing this ... stop having sex."

I raised my eyebrows. The timing was awkward. Wrapped in a sheet, I sat and listened. I didn't understand at first, but he explained to me how God's plan, for sexual relationships, is for it to be enjoyed in the context of marriage. Corwin knew this all along, but he had conveniently kept it from me until he felt so guilty about what he was doing that he couldn't live with himself. The more he shared, the more I realized that God's boundaries in this area are not meant to keep us from having fun but to protect us from the emotional, physical, and spiritual pain that comes with having sex outside of marriage. I didn't have a *lot* of experience in this area, but I was already quite familiar with the grief that came along with it. Sex was one more thing I had used to get the love I was searching for. Still, even my nominal experience was enough to make me feel guilty and ashamed.

It amazed me that a young man could love God so much that he wanted to surrender every aspect of his life to him. I was impressed that Corwin cared so much about *my* purity before God that he shared the truth and refused to further take advantage of my naiveté. From that moment onward, we decided to abstain from sex. But our new commitment proved difficult to honor. We would sometimes find ourselves reverting back to our old ways. We'd take things too far and found it difficult to backtrack. It was an uphill battle, and there were times when we didn't want to fight.

Despite our battle for sexual purity, Corwin continued to demonstrate God's love for me. He was concerned about everything that concerned me, and that made it easier for me to talk about things that I had suppressed before. He knew my fears, my faults, and my desires, and he prayed about them all. By the end of my sophomore season, we were inseparable. We went to classes together, ate lunch together, studied together, and worked out together.

Corwin was also a staple at my home competitions, as were the other football players who had gymnast girlfriends. Corwin showed his true dedication to my gymnastics career when he and teammate Terry Tumey, whose girlfriend was also on the gymnastics team, worked up enough nerve to ask head coach of UCLA football, Terry Donahue, if they could support their girlfriends by attending nationals in Salt Lake City. To their surprise, Coach Donahue thought it was a great idea, even though it would mean missing two days of spring practice. Such a thing was unheard of.

My parents were there too, decked out in their UCLA sweatshirts, and right beside them was the man after my own heart. I looked at Corwin before each event and placed my hands together to remind him to pray. That was something completely new for me. I had never allowed anyone outside of my coaches and one teammate to enter my zone before. My zone was where I focused as I prepared to do my routine. There, I visualized perfection and psyched myself up so that I could perform well. But seeing Corwin brought me so much comfort that I became dependent on his support and prayers. With him there, I was more relaxed, and a smile replaced my usually serious scowl.

Going into my second NCAA championship was a lot less nerve-racking than it had been the first year. By then I had competed in many televised meets, so the cameras faded into the background. Though I was more relaxed with Corwin there, I was still very intense right up until the event. But now I prayed more than before. I knew that God was real and that he was interested in everything that concerned me, even a gymnastics meet. I focused on doing my best for God. He had given me this extraordinary gift. Now I had the opportunity to display it. I was no longer on a mission to just please the crowd. I was out there first and foremost to bring pleasure to God. What an honor!

The first day of competition went well for our team. I qualified for finals on floor, which meant I would have a chance to defend my title. Up until that point, I never dreamed I'd have a chance to win it a second straight time. But now there was a real possibility.

The more people talked about it, the more nervous I became. I went from competing out of a place of solitude and peace to the pressure-laced atmosphere I had experienced before. Here I was again, in the same arena, filled to capacity. They had supported me so graciously the year before, and they were expecting an encore. When people said things like, "Kimmie, do you realize you could win the floor title two years in a row?" I knew they were only trying to encourage me. But each word was an additional weight on my already heavy shoulders.

I was the last competitor of the meet, which gave me lots of time to think. Actually, it was too much time. I just wanted to get it over with. I watched a few other competitors, but I wanted to stay as focused as possible. As my turn grew near, I bowed my head and prayed. "Lord, thank you for this opportunity to do my 'thang' for you. I've done all I can to reach this point. All I ask is that you help me to do my very best." Thoughts of my parents arguing pushed their way into my mind, followed by anger. "He doesn't care," I heard my mind saying. "But he's here!" came the reply. Over and over again I played a mental game of "he loves me, he loves me not." Although my father had flown out to see me contend, I couldn't help but think about the complaints and denigration I had to bear earlier that day and every time we were together.

Finally, I opened my eyes, only to find a television camera inches away from my face. My father shouts from the stands, "Let her concentrate!" If he could have, I'm sure he would have removed the cameraman himself.

I walked away from the cameraman and removed my sweats. I took a couple of deep breaths and jumped around to get my blood flowing. I felt sleepy. I always felt that way right before I went up. But I snapped out of it as my teammates cheered me on. Man, I loved those girls! Ms. Val put her face in mine and stared into my eyes. "This is *your* event, Kimmie," she said. "You know what to do."

I turned around with head held high, shoulders pulled back, and walked up to the edge of the floor mat, careful not to step across the line before I signaled the judge. Directly across from me, I spotted Momma, Daddy, and Corwin in the stands. Corwin motioned with his hands to indicate he was praying. I nodded slightly and smiled. "Lord, help me make them proud!" Then the judge's flag went up, my signal to take the floor.

All at once, my nervousness melted away. I stepped into character, no worries or fears clouding my mind, just one minute and thirty seconds of fun. I chose my starting position based on where the head judge was sitting. I wanted to be sure that at a certain point in my routine I could look her dead in the eye to show her just how much fun I was having. Ms. Val had choreographed an amazing routine that pushed the envelope when it came to my performance. I broke the "fourth wall" as I connected with the judges and the audience. I desperately needed the energy I drew from their smiles and cheers. My tumbling passes were flawless. As I neared the end of my routine, the thin air of Salt Lake City made itself known once again. My lungs burned. My mouth was dry.

Finally, there was only one last tumbling pass and it would all be over. The cheering ramped up from my team, and the audience jumped in. Boy, did it help. My body knew what to do, but would I have enough energy to do it? "Lord…" is all I had the strength to say. He filled in the rest. Round-off, flip-flop. As I bounded from the mat, I needed to get my arms up to give me enough momentum. But they were so heavy. Everything felt as though it was going in slow motion. Not sure how high I was, I remembered what Jim used to tell me: "When in doubt, tuck it out!" So I grabbed behind my knees and pulled as if my life depended on it. My fingernails dug deep into my skin. I rotated once in the air, saw the ceiling, the floor, the ceiling again, and then the floor coming fast! Tuck it out! Tuck it out! And land. I was on my feet. Yes! I did it! After a few short dance moves, I held my ending pose for what seemed like forever. It may have looked dramatic, but in reality, I was too tired to move.

As I stood there, relief flooded my system. I didn't care whether I had won or not. I was just glad it was over. I signaled the judges with a grateful smile and ran off the floor to meet my coaches. After a big hug from Jerry and Val, I turned to Momma and Daddy and held four fingers in the air. Then I pointed to them from across the arena. For you! In that brief gesture I thanked them for all they had done and let them know how much they meant to me. While looking at them, I noticed that everyone around them was standing. I worked my eyes around the arena and realized the entire audience was standing and cheering. I was so embarrassed I didn't know what to do.

"They want you out there, Kimmie," Ms. Val said. So I ran out to the middle of the floor, waving and smiling. Wow! I couldn't believe it. While I was out there, the scores went up—and so did the volume. Evidently, they all knew what I needed to score in order to win, a 9.8. And that's exactly what I got.

"You did it, Kimmie!" Jerry yelled from the sidelines. I covered my face with my hands as tears flooded my eyes. Then I looked up to where my parents were sitting and flashed my four fingers and pointed at them again, mouthing the words, "For you!"

I gave a final wave to the crowd then ran over to Jerry and Val. They embraced me with such love. They knew I could do it. Like the Shaws, they believed in me even when I didn't.

Returning back to UCLA afterward was a bit overwhelming. There were huge pictures in the papers. People whispered and pointed as I passed by. The students in the dorms asked questions I had no answers for, like, "What does it feel like to be the two-time national champion?" "Fine," was my usual response. Then I'd change the subject. Other people suddenly wanted to be friends. But when they introduced me by spouting my gymnastics résumé, I figured out pretty quickly that it wasn't me they cared about—it was my achievements and what they could gain by being associated with me.

But apart from that, what a year it had been. Not only had I defended the floor exercise title, but I had a new relationship with God and the man of my dreams.

# NINETEEN

# DEFENDING THE TITLE

During the first quarter back at school for my junior year, I found out that my teammate Jill had gone to the athletic director and requested that they pay for her books. They agreed, so I decided to ask them to do the same for me. I explained how I had signed on with UCLA believing that my scholarship included books. I shared my financial situation and reminded them of how well I was doing by bringing home national titles and All-American honors. My argument convinced them, and they agreed to pay for my textbooks for my junior and senior years. That lifted a lot of weight off my shoulders, and my grades went up substantially as a result.

But not everything was going quite as well. Corwin and I continued to battle with sexual purity. We had stopped going "all the way," but we struggled with going too far. We were too undisciplined with how much time we spent together and did not set up appropriate boundaries to protect ourselves when our passions were aroused. As a result of this, we broke up several times before finally calling it quits. My coaches were not too happy with the timing of our breakup, which happened a couple of weeks before nationals.

They knew how devastated I was when I broke up with my last boyfriend, and they were worried this would have a negative effect on my performance as well. They had also fallen in love with Corwin and were sorry to see him go. But I assured them that everything would be okay. Although I was no longer with the person who introduced me to God, I continued to go to church and grow in my faith. I chose not to hang around the mutual friends Corwin and I had, and as a result, I didn't have much of a Christian influence when it came to my acquaintances.

That year, 1989, nationals took place in Athens, Georgia. Expectations for our team were higher than ever. We were the favorites to win the team title, and once again, we would perform before a sold-out crowd. We were relaxed and excited about the day to come. Even I, "Miss Serious," was able to let down my hair. Tanya Service, Jill Andrews, and I were the gym clowns. During warm-up we lip-synched "R-e-s-p-e-c-t" by Aretha Franklin. I was Aretha and they were my backup singers. We even choreographed a sweet dance routine to the song. The three of us had grown close through the years. Tanya, at some points, would be the only one who could talk to me before an event. She always knew how to calm me down. I don't know what I would have done without her.

Because UCLA was ranked number one going into nationals, we got to compete in Olympic order: vault, bars, beam, and floor. As a team, our vaulting was strong. We had amazing scores that kept us solidly on top. There was such a strong connection with each of us that it was as if we were one person. We encouraged each other and reprimanded each other when necessary. I had never known such a cohesive group of women who genuinely loved each other and wanted the best for one another.

On uneven bars, our pace continued. I felt so strong and in shape. I performed one of my best routines, nailing the dismount without a wobble. "Thank you, Father," I said as I walked off the mat and into the waiting arms of my teammates. Then I sat down and spent some time in prayer. At first, it had been difficult to think of God as my Father because of my skewed view of the term. Yet, by that point, I had become more and more dependent on God. My trust in him had increased, and I realized that with him, all things are possible. So I wanted to thank him not only for a great routine but also for everything that led up to it. For me, each routine had a lifelong story behind it that could never be forgotten.

When I watched the video playback later, I realized that the play-by-play announcer for the meet, James Brown (current host of *The NFL Today* on CBS), chose to highlight my time of prayer. As I sat there with my head bowed and hands folded, the camera zoomed in to a close-up of my face. "Kim Hamilton, prayerfully giving thanks," he announced. Fade to black. Commercial break.

Our team was still on top as we proceeded to beam. To maintain our position, we couldn't have any falls. The first few routines went well. Then, right before I was to go up, one of my teammates fell and was injured.

Suddenly, the pressure was on. *Stay on the beam,* I told myself. *That's all you have to do.*

I mounted the beam with perceived ease. The bruises on my heels yielded sharp pains, but there was no time to think about that. The show had to go on. I had to be intentional with every move so that I stayed on the beam. Split jump on the beam sideways...check. Back handspring, back layout...check. Dance, dance, leap, front tuck...ouch! My bruises were killing me, but I was almost home free. Set up for the dismount. Back handspring step out to double back tuck. I didn't want to land short, so I pulled just a little harder than I should have. Suddenly, I realized I was rotating too fast.

I landed on my feet, but my center of gravity was moving backward. I stepped back with my right leg to catch myself, but my foot slipped out from under me, and I landed in a James Brown split. A five-tenth deduction. Ugh! I was almost there. The pain of having to stand up and signal that judge, knowing that this could cost the team the championship, was heart-wrenching. I ran over to my teammates and offered an apology. Even though they were down, they still supported me. "It's all right, Kimmie."

Our last event was floor. Due to our falls on beam, we had a lot of ground to make up. Thankfully, floor was one of our strongest events. Each of my teammates competed with grit and determination, knowing we were the closest we'd ever been to winning the national championship as a team. One by one, we hit our routines. I was the last to go. I didn't know it at the time, but for us to win, I had to score a perfect ten.

I took the floor my usual way, determined not to let my teammates down again. I hit my first and second tumbling passes and worked my way through the extended dance portion of the routine. The most difficult dance move was my triple turn. Not many gymnasts attempted it in competition. It was one of those moves that could make you or break you. I pulled my arms into the first turn. Then, during the second rotation, I felt my body leaning to one side. No matter how hard I tried to pull myself upright, the laws of physics were against me. I finished the turn leaning to the left, which threw me off balance. Instead of finishing the turn sharply leaning forward, I was forced to take a hop to the side. I did my best to cover up the mistake, but I knew it was a potential deduction.

I tried to forget about the mistake and carry on by making the most of what was left of my routine. I still smiled and played with the crowd, but that one little error loomed in my heart. Was it enough to make my team lose? I ran for my final double back, which was high, clean, and easy to land. All that was left was a pose. I misjudged my music, so I was a few seconds ahead and had to improvise by adding an extra head turn. But I was done. Now our fate was in the hands of the judges.

The first thing Ms. Val said when I got back to the sidelines was, "Great job, Kimmie! What was that little head thing on the end?" She knew it wasn't a part of the choreography. The whole team was excited about the possibility of winning, but each of them knew that the triple turn might be the deal breaker. Just then, the judges around the floor began to flash the scores. One judge gave me a 9.8, another a perfect ten. But when the average came out, it was not enough. We missed out on the title by a score of 0.05. We would have to settle for second place. As we took the podium to receive our silver medals, we smiled, but falling short by such an incredibly slim margin tore us up inside.

I qualified for finals on floor and vault, which took place on the following day. I was excited to make vault finals for the first time, but the only catch was that we had to compete two completely different vaults. I didn't feel prepared at all, so I had to dig *deep* and pull out a vault I had competed before graduating high school and only practiced on occasion while in college. It was a handspring half-turn followed by a back tuck. Unlike my handspring front tuck, I would land facing the vault. Jerry was amazing when it came to spotting. He could snatch a gymnast out of midair to keep her from killing herself. So I trusted him with my life. If I got into trouble, I knew he would save me.

First, I did "timers," practice vaults where I did a handspring half-turn without the back tuck. I went at it as hard as I could then landed on my back on the soft, squishy mats. That way, I knew I could, at least, make it around that far. Even so, when it came time for me to warm up for the actual vault, I was still very scared. If only I could go back to the Wooden Center and practice for a few more hours. Since that wasn't possible, my only choice was to go for it.

Jerry stood on a stack of mats right behind the horse so he could reach me. "Let's go, Kimmie!" he said. "Lord, please keep me safe," I prayed. Then I ran down the runway as fast as I could. I hit the horse, and my body flew into the air, turning and flipping then ... *bam!* I landed right on my face. *Okay. That wasn't so bad.* At least the first one was over with. Jerry gave me a few pointers; then it was on to the next one.

I was determined to take my time and push through the horse before I turned and tucked. *Don't rush it,* I told myself. "Help me, Lord," I prayed. Then I ran toward the horse and launched myself into the air again. This time I pulled it around and landed on my feet, with Jerry's help. Afterward, I laughed at myself. I couldn't believe I had to do this! Jerry continued to reassure me, as was his nature. Finally, my time ran out. The real competition was upon us.

The plan was for me to do my sure shot vault first and then move on to my secret weapon. It was a secret all right, even to me.

On my first vault, I ran down the runway, did a handspring front tuck, and ... stuck the landing. Yes! I signaled the judges then walked over to Jerry.

"You can't get better than that," he said.

As I walked back to the far end of the runway for my second vault, my mood was surprisingly light. So was that of the other finalists. They knew what I was up against with the second vault because they were up against it too. So instead of being stressed, we all just laughed about it. I still had to compete on floor afterward, so my only concern was to not injure myself. Landing short on this type of vault could do serious damage to my ankles, which were already a chronic source of pain. "Lord, keep me safe," I prayed. I had memorized a verse that helped me deal with my fears, so I began to repeat the first portion of it until the judges were ready for me. "God has not given (me) a spirit of fear."

When their flag went up, I signaled my readiness then glanced down at my foot to ensure it was in the right place. I took a deep breath, and then off I went. As I ran, I saw Jerry squatting to the right of the horse just out of the judges' way. He was ready to jump in if things took a turn for the worse, as they had during warm-ups. In warm-ups I had shown no indication that I could nail this vault on my own. Only God knew what would happen this time.

I hit the springboard harder than ever, knowing I needed all the explosion I could get. I made sure I also pushed off the horse like there was no tomorrow. I flew into the air and did a half-turn with my body outstretched. Then I drove my chest up and backward and pulled my knees in so tight my fingernails dug into my already scarred flesh.

As I rotated, I saw the ground coming up fast and knew immediately that I was lower than I should be. All I could do was tuck it out and…*bam!* I nailed it! I stood up straight with a curious look on my face as I realized what I had just done. Then my face was engulfed by a huge smile as I saluted the judges. I gave a quick jump for joy then ran straight to Jerry, who was just as excited as I was. Unbelievable! As I put on my warm-ups, the judges flashed my score, a 9.75. Only then did I realize I had just become the 1989 NCAA National Vault Champion.

When they called my name to receive the trophy, I congratulated the others then took my place on the podium. I looked over at Jerry and remembered just how far I had come over the past few years. As a freshman, I was the weakest vaulter on the team. Now I was the national champion. God was showing me that with faith and perseverance, the unimaginable could become a reality.

My moment of victory was short lived, however, because almost immediately I had to focus on floor. I needed to stay warm and loose. So while I waited, our trainer massaged me to try to get the kinks out. I did some stretching and worked on that triple turn so that I would not experience the same fate I had encountered during the last round.

The competition on floor was fierce. Every gymnast was incredible. There was no way the judges were going to hand me this title. I had to earn it. And yet, unlike the previous year, I came in wanting this title more than anything.

My music was an eclectic mixture of African instruments composed especially for me. It told a story of mystery and intrigue. Most gymnastics choreographers focus only on body and head movement, but Ms. Val choreographed everything from my eyes right down to the tips of my fingers and toes. No part of my body was allowed to be out of character. My routine went against all that was standard. I flexed my feet, used my hips, stopped suddenly, moved quickly, and fell gracefully. It was an incredible combination that kept the audience guessing as to what I would do next. While performing the routine, I felt more like an artist than an athlete. Yet the two always worked hand in hand.

As usual, I chose my starting position so I could have the most eye contact with the judges. After signaling them with a genuine smile, I got into character and took my place at the corner of the mat. My face stoic, I stared at a woman in the crowd who was directly in my line of sight. She and those around her began to fidget, probably wondering if they should move or sit perfectly still so I wouldn't be distracted. To me, it didn't matter. I wanted them to become part of what I was doing, not mere spectators. I wanted them to know that I saw them and that they were special, even without me using words.

The music finally started, and I slowly turned my head to scan the crowd. I distinctly moved my body to a number of musical notes that left me in a balanced lean, the same stoic expression upon my face. Then, after three startling hits on the djembe drum, I took off and tumbled a round-off flip-flop double-pike into a nice landing. Finally, it was time to smile. I worked my dance moves, intentionally looking at the people in the audience. When I reached the far corner, I flashed a smile at three guys who were standing there then turned to do my second tumbling pass. When I turned, the three of them grabbed their hearts and fell over backward. Everyone saw it but me.

I was so focused and having so much fun that I did my second tumbling pass with ease. As I danced, my face changed to fit the mood of the music. No one in my line of sight was immune to my looks and stares.

Finally, I reached my triple turn. *Here we go, Kim,* I said inside. *You can do this.* I squared my shoulders, positioned my feet, then went up on my toes as I began to spin. One...two...three...yes! Where was that yesterday? Stop. Focus. *Father, please help me make this last pass.*

I danced into the corner doing a tour jeté, landing in a squatting position. I popped up into a corner pose and winked at the first person I saw, who happened to be a sports reporter standing in the corner. *Wow, he's really cute,* I thought. *Focus.* I turned once more and took a deep breath. *Lord, help me!* I ran down the mat and completed my double back tuck without a flaw.

As soon as I landed, I heard cheers rise up from the audience. One last move, and I was finished. *Thank you, Father; you are so good!* I signaled the judges and ran over to meet my coaches.

"Ten! Ten! Ten! Ten!" the audience chanted with fervor. "Ten! Ten! Ten! Ten!" It got louder with every breath. All eyes were on the judges. Finally, the first judge held up her score, a perfect ten. The audience cheered. Then the second judge—another ten. The cheers intensified. The next judges each gave me a 9.8, which dropped the average down to a final score of 9.9.

When the head judge flashed the final score, the cheers were replaced by boos. "She was robbed!" I heard someone say. "What, are they blind?" I heard from another. I merely shrugged. It wasn't a perfect score, but it was still good enough to win the national floor exercise title. Yet it wouldn't be my title alone. I shared it with Corrinne Wright.

Corrinne was one of the other black gymnasts I competed against when I was younger. Who would have thought there would ever be not one but two black women in this position? When we met at the podium, I wrapped her up in a huge hug and swung her around. Then we smiled and waved for the cameras. What a great ending to my third year with the Bruins. Corwin wasn't out there in the crowd, but at least Momma and Daddy were. And they couldn't have been prouder of their little girl.

---

Once again, though, despite my success, I was still incredibly lonely. Due to my shyness, I still had a difficult time making new friendships, and soon I was isolated once again. In my brief moments of free time, I went on long drives and explored Los Angeles. I found a great place on a hilltop where I could see a panoramic view of the city. I'd go there late at night when I was sad and talk to God. The city lights twinkled through my tears as I poured out my heart to him. I shared my desires and dreams, my delights and disappointments. It became my personal meeting place with God.

I also spent many nights reading the Bible. The words seemed to come alive like never before. I fell asleep every night to the sound of a Christian radio station. Messages from God's Word lulled me to sleep at night and were the first thing I heard in the morning. It gave me a sense of peace and quelled my loneliness for a spell.

I told a few people how lonely I was, but for some reason they never believed me. They laughed it off, thinking I was just being funny. But I felt as though I was in a glass box surrounded by thirty thousand students. I could see them, and they could see me, and though the glass barrier protected me from hurt, it also isolated me from love. I knew in my heart that this God I had come to love was there for me, but I needed company from someone I could see and touch.

One day I ran into a guy I had met during my freshman year. He asked if I was going to a big party that was happening that night. I had not heard about the party, but since it was a Friday night and I had nothing else to do (as usual), I decided to go...alone. It was my freshman year all over again.

When I arrived, I saw a lot of football players I knew, including some with whom I attended Bible study. Upon seeing me, they hid their beers behind their backs. To make them feel even more uncomfortable, I went over to talk to them to see how long they could keep up the appearance. By the way they acted, you would have thought I was their mother. After I got my kicks by cramping their style, I stood over in a corner and did my best not to make it too obvious I was there alone.

Suddenly, two guys swept into the party. Everyone seemed to know them, including my athlete friends. These guys weren't athletes, though. One of them made his way to my corner and greeted me. All I remember were his thick eyebrows, diminutive eyes, and the biggest smile I'd ever seen. "I saw you on TV," he said. "You're the gymnast, right?"

"Yes," I responded hesitantly. He introduced himself as "John" and his friend as Cuba. We talked for a few minutes before the two of them continued on their rounds as if the world could not go on without them.

I kept thinking how familiar John seemed, as if I had met him before, but I couldn't put my finger on where. Finally, I asked one of the football players. He mumbled something about John and his friend being into acting. So I figured they were theater majors and I must have seen them somewhere on campus.

Afterward, I walked around, danced a little bit, and then finally decided to go home. As I was walking out, John followed me outside and offered to walk me to my car. We spent a long time talking in the parking lot. The conversation was free and easy, not awkward at all. We exchanged numbers; then off I went. I found it fascinating that finally a normal (non-athlete) guy was interested in me. What a nice thought. Maybe there was hope for me after all.

# TWENTY

# CHOOSING GRACE

Having just come off my third consecutive national floor exercise title and adding a national vault title as well, I spent the summer working to maintain an ideal weight and preparing for my senior season. I was excited about finishing my career at UCLA strong and defending the floor title for the fourth time. But I also couldn't shake the feeling that I would sustain an injury before the year was out. I even mentioned it to my trainer in September of 1989. For me, the scariest part of an injury was the initial pain. So I prayed that if I did get injured, the pain would be minimal.

Despite my fears, my training went well during my senior year. Finally, it came time for us to compete in our big home meet at Pauley Pavilion, the *Los Angeles Times* Invitational. It was February 1990. The *Times* ran advertisements with my picture and the caption "Amazing Grace." I don't know what the advertisers were thinking, but for me this caption epitomized the amazing grace God had shown me when he called me out of my difficult circumstances and into his loving arms.

That year I had really improved on vault. My handspring front was higher than ever, and it was as if everything had finally clicked. Quite a few times, though, I was higher than I thought and wound up landing with my body totally straight, which caused my head to whip back. As a result, I began to have massive headaches and neck aches. Sometimes the pain would shoot up through my head as I walked across campus and stop me dead in my tracks. The surrounding muscles in my neck and upper back constantly knotted up, creating the need for massages between every event.

I had another one of those landings while warming up for the *LA Times* Invitational. This time I blacked out and stumbled off the mat. Jerry asked if I was okay, but I shrugged it off. He reminded me to look for the landing and to bend my knees. I nodded then walked back to the end of the runway and put on my warm-ups. As I waited for my turn, all I could think of was my landing. *Please, God, help me stick it.*

When my turn came, I looked for my chalk mark on the floor among all the others. If I didn't start exactly on that mark, I would misstep and ruin my vault. Once I found my place, I put my toe on it. When I glanced up at the judge, her flag was already raised. I signaled that I was ready then stared down the vault horse as if it were the enemy. There was no way I would let it conquer me. I took a deep breath, rocked back onto my heels, and then took off.

I ran just fast enough so I could have full control when I hit the springboard. Then I swung my arms into the horse and pushed through my shoulders, bounding into the air. I tucked and rotated. I was so conscious about my landing that I held my tuck just a bit too long and had to step forward when I landed. I grunted in anger then turned to the judges with a fake smile pasted onto my face.

As I walked back to the far end of the runway for my second attempt, I heard Jerry's reassuring words. "You can do this, Kimmie. Nail it!" I nodded then quickly took my place. My teammates yelled, and the crowd cheered. *I can do this. Stick! Stick it!* I said to myself.

The judge's flag went up. I signaled and then set my feet. I looked at the horse again, this time with a smile. *I will conquer you.* I visualized a perfect vault. Then off I ran. This time I hit the springboard, launched myself off the horse, flew through the air while tucking my body, and then opened up at the perfect time. This time I didn't wobble at all on the landing. I even stood there for a few moments to emphasize that point. And this time the smile I showed the judges was real.

Jerry high-fived me, and my teammates welcomed me with hugs. To top it off, a small group of gymnasts in the stands made up a little chant in my honor. I waved at them as I put my grips on for the uneven bars, which was my next event. That made them scream all the more.

During my warm-up on the bars, I opened up on my staldter too early and fell off. That didn't exactly boost my confidence. I tried to shake it off. All that mattered was that I correctly executed it during the routine. My achievement on vault was important, but bars was one of my stronger events, so I was expected to contribute here as well.

I was slated to compete last for our team. For UCLA to stay on top, I couldn't afford a fall. Normally, this wouldn't be a problem. But for some reason my staldters were off, and everyone knew it. Would I be able to pull it off this time?

While I hopped up and down to warm up, Jill prepared the bars for me, caking water and chalk onto them until it was just the right consistency. She was the only one I trusted to do them right. If the bars were too wet and goopy or too dry, I could slip right off. When she was done, she gave me a nod of assurance and mouthed the words, "Come on, Kimmie. You can *do* this!" The look on her face was so intense that I thought if I didn't do it, she would personally jump me afterward and beat me up.

I took my place in front of the bars and signaled the judges, still smiling at the thought of Jill beating me up in a dark alley. Then I took a deep breath, and the smile was gone. I mounted the bar and began to swing through my routine. My first release was a Jaeger from an eagle grip, which I made easily. My next release was a Delchev. I went from a kip to a handstand (facing the low bar) with a half pirouette (half turn). But my pirouette was different from everyone else's. When I turned, I rotated on one hand while waving my other hand 360 degrees around from one side of the bar to the other (I perfected this move while working with Daddy several years back). It looked as if I was waving at the audience. And instead of finishing the turn on top of the bar, I fell past vertical with my hand still in the air then crossed it over my support hand at the last second. Then I swung under the bar while doing another half turn and driving my feet into the air. At the apex of my swing, I let go of the bar, flipped forward, and then caught the bar again. Who said you could only show style on floor or beam?

I caught my second release and continued nicely. As I kipped from low bar to high bar, I began to focus on my staldter. I knew I couldn't open up early like I had in warm-ups, but I had to hit a handstand for it to count. Handstand…swing…staldter…to a handstand! I had done it! Now one more. *Lord, help me!* Staldter…*uh-oh.* I opened up just a hair too early and was stuck in a slightly arched handstand on the high bar. If I didn't fight for it, I would fall. So I fought.

I heard, "Oohs!" from the audience and saw the judges out of the corner of my eye, leaning to the side, trying to help me from afar. I couldn't keep from smiling at the sight. I also caught a flash of my teammates leaning and holding onto each other. What was that sound? Was someone actually trying to blow me in the right direction? Whatever it was, it was working. Back in full control, I tightened my body and brought my toes down to the bar, swinging into my toe-on front with a half-twist. I hit the mat and…stuck the landing. Everyone went wild. Smiling with relief, I signaled the judges then ran into the waiting arms of my coaches and teammates.

While I removed my grips, I heard the group of young gymnasts in the audience yell in unison, "Let's go, Kim!" No doubt, they had coaxed their parents into bringing them to the meet.

Then I picked up my bag and moved over to the next event, balance beam. It was my favorite event to practice but my worst event to compete. I don't know why, but I always tensed up during competition. I would try so hard not to fall that I'd end up falling anyway.

My warm-up went fairly well, so I felt good. Right before I went up for my routine, Ms. Val gave me one of her famous pep talks to help me relax. Then I signaled the judges and mounted the beam with a front somersault. I made it, but I was unusually nervous and felt very awkward. Each difficult skill I performed was followed by a major wobble. I tried my best to pull it together, but it just wasn't happening. I managed to dismount without falling, but I knew my wobbles would count against me. I was very upset with myself. I knew I could do better, but apparently it was not my day. After sulking for a few minutes, I forced myself to let it go. I had to focus on my final routine for the night, floor exercise.

I had to run to catch up with my teammates, who were already walking over to the head judge's table. I joined them just in time to hear her say, "Good luck, ladies." Then we had three minutes to warm up. As I practiced my double backs, I felt energized and ready to go. This would be my opportunity to make up for my awful beam routine. The last tumbling pass I needed to warm up was my middle pass. I did a Russian front step-out front handspring, front layout with a half-twist, bounding into a straddle jump, punch-front, and then went back in the opposite direction into a round-off, flip-flop back layout step-out. Even though the layout step-out was a simple skill, it was a crowd pleaser because of the height I attained and the way I split my legs while rotating in a layout position.

Whenever we warmed up our tumbling passes, we alternated from one corner of the mat to the other in an X. To get as many turns as possible, the girl in one corner would start her pass when the other person hit the spot where the two diagonals intersected. This made for some close calls at rapid speed, so it was important to keep the lines moving. If anyone stopped in the middle of the mat, there was usually a collision.

As I took off for my Russian, front flip on my tumbling pass, I heard a loud *pop* in my foot. I knew something was wrong, but my momentum had me going so fast I couldn't stop. When I landed, I cartwheeled out of the skill then quickly hopped out of the way of the next tumblers.

As I sat down on the edge of the mat, I was afraid to put any pressure on my foot. I figured a bone had popped out of place and that if I could pop it back in I could continue. My trainer rushed over to see what was wrong. I told her about the pop and asked if she could put it back in place. She felt around and massaged my foot a bit, but she couldn't feel any dislocated or broken bones.

I stood up to test my foot and discovered I could not put any weight on it at all. Until that moment, I felt no pain at all. But when I tried to stand on it, the pain was excruciating. Tears flooded my face as I realized I would not be able to finish the meet. My trainer helped me over to the chairs where our team was waiting to compete. They wrapped a large bag of ice around my foot and gave me some crutches. I was devastated. I had never been injured so badly that I could not finish a meet.

With my foot elevated and packed with ice, I took on the role of cheerleader for our team. I cried and cheered and cried again, wishing more than anything that I could be out there with them. During a lull in the competition, I heard the group of young gymnasts yell in unison, "We love you, Kim!" As I turned to see them all waving at me, the tears flowed all the more. "I love you too!" I yelled back. Then I grabbed my crutches and clumsily made my way over to them. Even though I was hardly able to see them through my tears, I sat down beside them and thanked each one of them for their support. One little girl pulled out a gold chain with half of a heart on the end.

"I want you to have this," she said.

"Oh, it's so pretty. I can't take this," I responded.

"But I want you to. It's a friendship necklace. Your heart fits into my heart, and we'll be friends forever," she said, pointing to the other half of the heart hanging around her neck.

"Thank you. This is the best gift I've ever gotten." I held the necklace like the priceless piece of jewelry it was. Then I gave her a huge hug and thanked her and the other girls again before hobbling back over to my teammates.

By the time the meet was over, the pain had become so unbearable that I couldn't keep from crying. I wasn't able to drive, so John took me home. The next day, he and Momma took me in to see the doctors. The prognosis was a severe separation of the first and second metatarsals (two of the five long bones in your foot). The doctors told me I would be in a cast for at least six weeks and that it was doubtful I would be able to come back in time for nationals, which were only two months away. I left the doctors with a new set of crutches and a pink cast. John bought me a pair of gray, purple, and pink hiking boots to go with my cast so I could look "fashionable" while hopping around.

---

I had spent quite a bit of time with John. We dated for over a year and had become the best of friends. Our relationship ranged from silly to serious and everything in between. There was lots of laughter and spontaneity, never a dull moment. We celebrated birthdays, new jobs, and even my graduation from UCLA. There was just one problem: he did not have the same desire to grow in a relationship with God that I did. I shared my faith with him and even took him to church. I thought I could be a positive influence on him, but instead, I found myself falling farther away from God. My newfound Christianity was no match for the influence he had on me. Eventually, I realized I would have to choose between John and Jesus.

I finally worked up the courage to do what I knew was right, which was to end the relationship. Although John found it hard to believe I could just walk away, he understood why I had to do it, and we amicably parted ways. It still took me a while to get over it, though. After all, I had just lost my best friend. But I knew in the long run, it was the best thing to do.

By the way, eventually I realized that John was not quite as "normal" as I first thought. The reason he looked so familiar to me that first night was because he was an actor who made his living doing television and movies. And his friend Cuba? Well, you may have heard of him. He went on to do some pretty spectacular things as well, such as winning an Oscar for his role in *Jerry McGuire.*

In June of 1990, I graduated from UCLA with a degree in sociology and an emphasis in psychology. Bobby and Jackie (Joyner-Kersee) extended an invitation for me to live with them while I transitioned into the real world, but I was anxious to be on my own. So I moved into a studio apartment on St. Andrews Place and Wilshire Blvd. I had been attending a Bible study with a group of women who met at Denny's on Hollywood Boulevard once a week. This group included legendary singers from Motown and known actresses from film, television, and stage. I was the youngest of the bunch, and I learned a great deal by being around these women and gleaning from their life lessons. Corine Duke was one of these women who became a mentor and close friend to me. I went to her about advice on relationships and personal growth, and she always spoke with a strong voice of wisdom. I longed to be close to God like she was, and I listened to her every word. She knew this and was careful to point me to the scriptures and emphasize my need to rely on God and not her. She knew that man will fail you but God will always be there. I enjoyed my times with Corine, but she was in a different stage of life than me. She was highly involved in her husband, George Duke's, music career, and they had two sons to care for. I desperately looked forward to our weekly meetings. These were usually the only times I wasn't isolated.

Sometimes I'd go alone to a nightclub in downtown LA. I'd find a group of people who were dancing together and join in. We'd take turns trying to outdo each other. Both my gymnastics and my dance training came in handy, as I had friendly battles with the famed hip-hop dancer, Shabadoo, from the 1984 movie *Breakin.'* Shabadoo was impressed with my skills and even taught me a few of his own moves. There were hours of laughter and fun, but it always ended with me going back to my empty art deco apartment, five stories above the Wilshire District. I often spent time on the fire escape watching the police helicopter shine their searchlight throughout the neighborhood. Or I'd sneak up to the rooftop, where I had an unobstructed view of the Hollywood sign.

Isolation led to loneliness, and loneliness led to me making some unwise decisions. I kept getting mixed up with the wrong people. I would enter into relationships I thought were genuine and end up getting hurt. I was naïve and a horrible judge of character. I would not recognize the ruthlessness and general disregard of the people I was around until I had invested my emotions, and by then it was too late. I was already hurt. After this happened repeatedly, I finally woke up and decided that the best thing to do was walk away. I removed myself from my circle of "friends" in an effort to start over. I knew that I needed to surround myself with like-minded people. I couldn't stand alone and hope to live a life that honored God. I became more careful about who I allowed into my life, which meant distancing myself from those whose company I once enjoyed. It was difficult, but I knew I had to do it.

I prayed every day, crying out to God for help. During those prayer times, I got the strong sense that if I didn't change the course of my life immediately, it would drift in a direction that would eventually destroy me. As always, the choice was between immediate satisfaction and God's lasting peace. Was I willing to risk everything God had in store for me in exchange for the happiness of the moment, or was I willing to wait and trust in him? I decided to take my chances with God.

> Those who cling to worthless idols forfeit the grace that could be theirs.
>
> Jonah 2:8 niv

I took a job as a gymnastics coach while I tried to figure out what I *really* wanted to do with my life. During my time off, I spent countless hours reading the Bible. I also became more involved in church and volunteered as a volleyball coach at a mission in downtown LA. I'd show up at 4:00 p.m. to the rundown old building. I'd wade through the homeless men who were hanging around outside waiting to receive food, clothing, shelter, or all three. Their skin was caked with dirt, teeth rotting, hair matted, open lesions on their arms and legs from injuries that were never taken care of properly. Their clothing was layers of ripped and holey garments, grayish brown with dirt, the same color of their skin. The men got used to seeing me there. "Hey, hey!" I would greet them. "Hey darlin,' how you doin' today?" they usually chimed in return. And if there was a new guy around and he tried to get fresh or be disrespectful to me, the others would quickly put him in his place. This was usually followed by an apology from the newbie. I'd go inside and coach these, many times, homeless children who obviously were not cared for properly. It could have been due to a neglectful parent or the minimal amount of resources available to them. Some were definitely troubled, but others just wanted to be loved. That's where I came in. I received no recognition, no pay, and very little thanks for this role, but the feeling of giving to others gave me a high that was different from anything I had ever experienced. And the peace that I had was priceless.

Once my foot was completely healed, I began to look for a better way to end my gymnastics career. With much prayer, I felt that I was supposed to start training again. I decided my best target was the 1992 Olympics. When I presented the idea to my former coaches at UCLA, they agreed to help out. One of my coaches, Scott Bull, even volunteered to use his own personal time to whip me back into shape.

One day while walking to the training room, I ran into Corwin, whom I had not seen for several months. He was on crutches, having just undergone knee surgery. We exchanged pleasantries then discussed his injury. He was a senior that year with hopes of an NFL career, so he was praying the injury wouldn't mean an end to that dream. When we ran out of things to talk about, things got a little awkward, so we quickly said our good-byes then continued about our business. At the time, I didn't really think much about it, except that I hoped he would recover. Only later did I realize that chance meeting was the spark that would eventually rekindle our friendship.

My workouts were tough because I had not done gymnastics in quite a few months. I worked tirelessly doing many repetitions, but after a while Scott sat me down and broke the news—he didn't think I could make it. I had made some progress, but not nearly as quickly as he expected. His words stung so badly. I walked away with tears streaming down my face. I couldn't understand. Had I heard God wrong?

As I walked to the restroom to collect myself, I saw a notice on the wall for a group called Athletes in Action. They were looking for some gymnasts to go on a tour in Asia. Despite my tears, I couldn't help but smile. Maybe I had heard God right after all. I *was* supposed to start training again, just not for the Olympics. If I hadn't been training, I would never have seen the flyer or been in adequate shape.

I signed up for the trip then immediately started raising funds. I had never raised money on my own before, but God provided generously through friends, family, and people from my church. During the one-month trip, we would travel to Korea, Japan, Okinawa, and Taiwan. I didn't know what would be expected of me on the trip, so I made sure I was ready to do routines on every event.

Since I was spending more time on campus again, I kept running into Corwin. One day he asked me out to dinner. I accepted, but only because I didn't know how to say no. He took me to a wonderful Cuban restaurant called Versailles. It was a little awkward because we didn't really know what to say to each other, but he was on his best behavior. Meanwhile, I struggled with how to be cordial without giving him the impression I was interested in anything more than a friendship. The previous feelings I had for him were no longer there. Thankfully, the night ended with no major hitches. I thanked him for the evening and went home.

After that, Corwin continued to call me from time to time, our conversations becoming more comfortable. I even took him to my secret lookout where I still went to meet with God when I was feeling down. We stared out at the city below, which helped both of us relax. As the conversation flowed, we talked about what God was doing in our lives and how we were growing in our faith.

Then something really strange happened. In the midst of our conversation, we realized we were both having the same recurring dream. I told Corwin what happened in my dream, and then he described the next part of his dream, which also happened to be the next part of my dream. We went back and forth like that three or four times until the dream finally came to an end. We each dreamed of ourselves being chased down what seemed to be an unending, spiraling flight of stairs. The first dreams would stop before we got to the bottom. In the final dream we reached the bottom, and standing there was a man in a white robe and sandals who rescued us from whatever it was that was chasing us. I could see his entire body but not his face. Afterward, we stared at each other, marveling at how weird it all was. Inside, I couldn't help but think that maybe I was becoming more interested in Corwin than I wanted to admit.

Sure enough, as we started to see each other more often, my affection for Corwin began to return. Then it was suddenly time to leave for Asia. The mission trip was an incredible experience. I met other gymnasts from around the country who also had a strong faith in God, and we all used our sport to tell others about him. We did exhibitions before hundreds and sometimes close to a thousand people at a time. Afterwards, we'd take the mic and share our stories of how we met God and give others the opportunity to get to know him as well.

Many of the people there practiced Buddhism. There were small but elaborate temples scattered throughout the cities, where people could enter and worship. Just about every house had its own shrine, a special room that was dedicated to worshipping their god. These shrines were perpetually lit by a red light, and at night as we drove to our next destination, we could see the red glow dotting the countryside.

The responses we received when we shared our faith were overwhelming. For many, it was their first time hearing about Christianity. As the audience learned about God's love and his desire to commune with them, they longed for the opportunity to get closer to their creator. In Japan, there was a girl named Mika who was fascinated with this God who was so accessible and cared for her as an individual. She would show up at our various events to see us perform and to hear our message again. Mika was never without a small gift for me. I was grateful for her kindness. She communicated that she wanted to trust in the God we served, but her parents were Buddhists and would not approve. Each time I saw her she seemed to be one step closer to trusting Jesus, but I never pushed her to do so. I merely displayed to her the love that Christ had shown me and accepted her just as she was. At the end of our trip, I saw Mika one last time. We both were very sad that we might never see each other again. Once more, she had a gift for me, but this one would be the greatest of them all. She delivered the news that she had trusted in Jesus and was now my sister in Christ.

In addition to speaking and performing, we got to work with children, teaching them gymnastics and choreographing routines for them to perform. Oh, the satisfaction that came with sharing my faith, giving encouragement, and helping people. It was an experience I didn't want to end. It was that same high I got while coaching volleyball at the LA Mission. I grew in so many ways. It was just the boost I needed to keep moving in the right direction. And yet, the entire time I couldn't stop thinking about Corwin. He wrote me a couple of letters, and I read them over and over again. The longer I was away from him, the more I wanted to be with him.

When I returned to LA, our romance was rekindled, but this time we took every precaution to keep our relationship pure. That meant not being together late at night and setting other boundaries that kept us from taking things too far. It was difficult, but being intentional about drawing the line in advance was a lot easier than scrambling to back things up after we had already crossed it.

As I grew closer to Corwin, my relationship with God grew as well. I became less selfish. I no longer desired to do things just to satisfy my own longings. I wanted to have a meaningful existence that included impacting the lives of others. I also had a paradigm shift in terms of what drew me to the opposite sex. For so long, I had been attracted to the bad boys, young men who were much like my father had been when he was younger. Remembering all the pain my mother had experienced, I decided to go with my head and be with a young man who loved God even more than he loved me. It was such a blessing to be in a relationship with someone like Corwin, who had the same desire to honor God with his life. In a sense, I had been a damsel in distress, and he became my knight in shining armor.

A few months after I returned from Asia, Corwin asked me to be his wife. I said yes, and six months later, we were married.

# TWENTY-ONE

# THE HONOR IS MINE

Back in my hotel room, I finished putting on my makeup and combing my hair. I was ready to commentate the gymnastics meet. Then, as I gathered my things to go out, my cell phone rang. It was Ms. Val. It had been ten years since she'd coached me at UCLA, and I always enjoyed hearing her voice. She had been such a good source of encouragement for me. We took a few minutes to catch up, but I sensed she had some exciting news to share. That's when she told me I was to be inducted into UCLA's Hall of Fame.

I was speechless. Despite my achievements, it never crossed my mind that I would receive such an honor. I couldn't believe it. My name would go alongside the likes of Jackie Robinson, Arthur Ashe, Jackie Joyner-Kersee, and countless other elite athletes. Amazing!

The Hall of Fame induction ceremony took place on October 21, 2000, a gorgeous Southern California day. I had never been to such an event before, so I had no idea what to expect. At my table were my former coaches Jerry Tomlinson and Valorie Kondos-Field, my good friend Corine Duke, my mother and her husband, James, and Corwin. I hadn't spoken to Daddy in a long while, and I didn't bother to let him know about the honor. I wasn't trying to exclude him purposely. He just wasn't in my life at the time, and telling him about it was not a natural thing for me to do.

As I sat at the table, I read my profile in the ceremony's program. It listed records that I didn't even know I had set. It also stated that I was "the first gymnast to win three-consecutive NCAA National Floor Exercise titles." All I could think was, *It should have been four*. That may sound arrogant, but it was just my perfectionist mentality kicking in. I had trained so long to be perfect, and a fourth consecutive title would have made the picture-perfect ending to my career. My attention shifted back to the ceremony. After basketball great Lucius Allen was inducted, it was my turn.

"Our next inductee was a UCLA gymnast who made NCAA history by becoming the first woman to win three straight NCAA individual titles on the floor exercise. She added a fourth individual NCAA crown in 1989 on the vault. On her way to both titles, Hamilton set NCAA records by scoring a 9.90 on floor and 9.75 on vault. While qualifying for the NCAAs, Hamilton won three straight NCAA West Regional titles in the all-around and also on floor. She also won consecutive Pac-10 titles in both the floor and uneven bars in 1988 and 1989. Overall, she was a six-time All-American. She is married to former UCLA football player Corwin Anthony. Please welcome Kim Hamilton Anthony."

I gave Corwin's hand a quick squeeze then stood up and made my way to the podium. Before I gave my acceptance speech, I looked out at the audience. Directly in front of me was 1960 Olympic gold medalist and UCLA Hall of Famer Rafer Johnson. Other Hall of Fame inductees were sprinkled throughout the room. My knees weakened at the thought of becoming part of this great fraternity. I took a deep breath then began my speech. "Little did I know when I was flipping on the brick sidewalks in Richmond, Virginia, that I would become a world-class gymnast and have the opportunity to be *recruited* by UCLA.

"Little did I know that my parents cleaning the gym at night and raising money by any means necessary so that I could afford to train as a gymnast would pay off with a scholarship to *attend* UCLA.

"And little did I know, when I was watching John Wooden as a child in the seventies lead his team to NCAA victories, that I would one day join him and the likes of Kareem Abdul-Jabbar, Jackie Robinson, and Arthur Ashe in this exclusive group that *is* the UCLA Hall of Fame.

"It is truly an honor to be part of such an amazing group of people who have had such a positive influence in the world of sports.

"My coaches had no idea of the personal struggles I faced while here at UCLA. In spite of my attitudes, they continued to believe in me, and they encouraged me to become the athlete I never thought I could be. When I couldn't dream, they dreamed for me. Thank you, Jerry and Ms. Val, for putting up with me and helping me to achieve so much while I was here at UCLA.

"Momma, you've been through so much, and you sacrificed in some unbelievable ways so that I could be where I am today. Without your endless support and encouragement, none of this would be possible.

"Corwin, you shared with me that which would become *the* most important thing in my life when you introduced me to a personal relationship with God. Thank you for not being afraid to share the truth with me and for supporting me through the tough times.

"And for those who have chosen me to receive such an honor, I thank you. I am incredibly grateful for this opportunity to be in the company of such gifted athletes and sports figures. God bless you all."

I walked back to the table thanking God for his mercy and grace. I knew that without him, nothing I accomplished would have been possible. As I sat down, I glanced once more at my list of accolades. In that moment, I suddenly realized my career-ending foot injury was actually a blessing in disguise.

You see, after the injury I continued to train on uneven bars and do as much as I could to maintain my strength, still hoping I would recover in time for nationals. However, two weeks out I was still in excruciating pain. Seeing my disappointment, Jerry sat me down and told me something that he hoped would ease my pain.

Back when the doctors had originally investigated my ongoing neck injury, they told my coaches that if I continued to snap my head back on my vault landings, it was highly possible that I could break my neck, become paralyzed, or even die. Jerry and the other coaches hadn't told me earlier because they didn't want to scare me.

It all made sense now. What I had regarded as a curse was actually a blessing from God that made it *impossible* for me to compete, thus preventing me from possibly doing permanent damage to my spine. Even though I continued to struggle with a lot of pain, I still had a fully functioning body. I had given birth to two wonderful boys, and I was able to enjoy life without any major physical boundaries.

Why had it taken me more than ten years to realize this, to recognize God's work in my life? The answer was simple: I was too busy focusing on myself, my desires, and what could have been. In that moment, however, I realized that God cared about me so much that he wanted to give me the very best, even if that meant suffering temporary disappointment. In the long run, he never disappoints.

Was it worth it? Was my gymnastics career worth the physical pain that I now experience? If I consider the life lessons of goal setting, perseverance, and discipline that I have applied to virtually every aspect of my life, then yes, it's all been worth it. If I think of how my mind broadened and my circle of influence grew from a city block to the entire world, then yes, it was worth it.

If I could go back and change one thing about my life, though, I would have started a personal relationship with God sooner. Then I would have been using my gift to honor him from the start instead of trying to gain fleeting honor for myself. I would have been more secure and confident, which would have made my career a lot more enjoyable.

But perhaps I *needed* to go through all that I did so that I could become better equipped to fulfill my purpose: to share with others how much God loves them, that he's created and gifted them for a special purpose, and that he can give them the strength to persevere through *any* circumstance. I am so passionate about this message because throughout the ups and downs of my life, I have found that it is only when we embrace these truths that we are ever *truly* successful and *truly* fulfilled.

## TWENTY-TWO

# RECONCILED

Today, when I travel around the country and share my story, the question I am asked most often is, "What ever happened to your father? How's he doing?" People wonder, "Do you get along, or are you enemies?"

For many years, I was not able to answer the questions about his welfare because I just didn't know. Over a period of several years, I tried reaching out to him, but my calls were never returned. My birthdays and Christmases went unrecognized. I was so saddened by this lack of communication that each holiday I fell into a deep depression. Would I call him again this year, knowing I wouldn't get a response? Could I handle the rejection one more time?

After God began to change me, he helped me forgive my father. But my father's continued unresponsiveness made me want to forget about him as well. I tried, but to no avail. I thought about him every single day. I wondered what he was doing, whether he was safe, and if he loved me. I wanted to hate him too, but my heart wouldn't let me do that either. So whenever he came to my mind, I asked God to either let me forget him or else make things all better. As time passed, he'd come to mind more and more. Finally, I asked God what he wanted me to do about it.

Early in the year of 2008, I believed God was telling me that he would not allow this book to progress without me reconciling with my father. I cried out, "But Lord, I've been trying to reconcile with him for years, but he won't even return my calls. I don't know what else to do. How long do I have to put myself through this?"

"How long did I wait for *you?*" came a voice in my heart.

"Nineteen years," I replied, my protests silenced with a single question.

From that point on, I began to pray about how God wanted me to contact Daddy. I asked him to prepare my heart so I could say the right things when the moment came. Several months passed, during which I did nothing but pray. God used that time to work on my heart so that I went from wanting my father to account for his actions to merely wanting him to know how much I loved him and how much he had always meant to me. I was not going to love him only if he loved me in return. I was going to love him no matter what. If God could love me no matter what I'd done, who was I to offer my father anything less?

Then one day my daddy's older brother called me out of the blue. I had not spoken to him for years, but we picked up as though it was just yesterday. He caught me up on the latest with his family and told me how much he cared about me. I couldn't believe my ears. I thought that Daddy's side of the family had forgotten about me. After reconnecting with Daddy's other two brothers as well, I realized that was not the case at all. They all cared about me and loved me. Suddenly, my heart began to hope again. Could Daddy feel the same way?

After the call with my uncles, I had a sudden urge to talk with Daddy. I wanted to call him, but I was scared. I got some counsel as to how I should approach the situation and decided to go back to Virginia for Thanksgiving in hopes of getting a chance to talk with him.

Finally, I worked up enough nerve to make the call. I had my notes beside me so I would not forget what I wanted to say. But when the answering machine picked up, my careful plans flew out the window. I stuttered my way through my message, letting him know that the boys and I would be in Richmond and that we wanted to see him. If he wanted to see us, he could call me and let me know. I also told him that I would understand if he didn't want to get together.

He called back that very night and left a message saying yes, he wanted to see us. I was happier than I had been in a long time. He ended his message with three powerful words: "I love you." I must have listened to that message fifteen times just to hear him say it over and over again.

Once we got to Virginia, I called to let Daddy know we were there. He took time off from work and spent the whole day with the boys and me at the Science Museum of Virginia. Daddy was in his element, still as excited and knowledgeable as ever. As the day passed, we grew more comfortable with each other.

That day I found out that for years Daddy has had a great job where he continues to excel. He owns his own home on an acre of land, where he has created the most beautiful gardens. He spends a lot of his time tending to his gardens and fixing up the house. As he demonstrated in the museum that day, he also continues to educate himself. I don't think there is any subject that he doesn't know *something* about.

Later that night, I talked to him about some of the things that took place when I was growing up and how they had affected me. He listened in silence as I poured my heart out to him. It was a very emotional time, full of painful moments. I also shared with him how God had changed my life and given me the ability to forgive and how now I was able to use the pain from my past to encourage others who have gone through similar experiences. I needed him to know that I was not sharing my story to embarrass him in any way, although I was sorry if it had.

I also told him that I tried to hate him over the years, but I was never able to pull it off. Each time, my love for him would burst forth and wash the hate away. The truth was that I loved him so much that if I had the chance to go back in time and choose my father, I would pick him all over again. I loved him, and I needed him to be part of my life.

Daddy didn't deny our past or blame anyone else for his behavior. He took full responsibility for his actions and apologized to me for the things he had done. His biggest concern was that in the articles he'd read about me, it seemed as if I was saying Momma supported my gymnastics career but he didn't. I assured him that even though I consider Momma to be my biggest cheerleader because of her continual presence in my life, I also recognized and shared about the support he gave me, when he was able to be there for me, that is. Hopefully this book has made that point even clearer.

The final question I had for Daddy was regarding how he felt about me sharing my story with others through this book. I knew it would be difficult for him to relive the past, even more so to have so many others know about it, so I was ready for him to let me have it. Instead, he told me he was glad I was sharing my story because it would help other people. Then he said those words I've longed to hear from him for years: "I'm proud of you, and I love you."

For the first time in many, many years, I finally felt like his little girl again. I love you, Daddy!

## TWENTY-THREE
# CONCLUSION:

---

### BEAUTIFUL HOPE

As surprising as it sounds, while growing up, I did not realize I was limited by lack of money, the color of my skin, or the address of my home. When I did become aware of it, I tried to bury my past and pretend it wasn't true. I just deleted it from my mind, put on my mask each day, and did my best to make myself "acceptable." My mask was infinitely moldable, allowing me to blend in just about anywhere. But my true face kept pushing through, and I finally grew weary of covering it up. It wasn't until my true self reached up and pulled me down with it that I was forced to face my past and the pain it had caused. Confronting it was the only way for healing to take place.

For such a long time, I looked for something that would fulfill my longing for meaning, purpose, and value. At first, I tried to find it by gaining love and acceptance from my earthly father. He was unable to give it fully, though, because of his struggles with his own issues. When that didn't work, I thought I could find it through gymnastics. Despite my success, something was still missing. So I thought a boyfriend or a better education or popularity would work. The list went on and on. Each time, I realized such things could only provide a temporary fix. I needed something permanent.

When I was made aware of the life of Jesus and what he came to do, I finally found what I was looking for all those years, a love that could not be earned, bribed, or bought. It is the type of love that only God can give. This love brings me a sense of hope and security that no earthly relationship or accomplishment can rival. God's love is the permanent solution to my every need. Even though I've failed time and again, he's never given up on me. I've always been able to go back to him for the strength and encouragement to start all over again. He understands my struggles and my weaknesses, and yet he still accepts me. No longer is my life a chain of unhappiness, guilt, and shame. I now live a life filled with a beautiful hope that no one can take away.

I pray my story has given you hope as well. We live in an age where encouragement and inspiration to achieve our God-given dreams is needed more than ever.

Would you allow me to share another story? This time it's not about me. It's about someone else who has brought the greatest encouragement and inspiration to my life.

## THE GREATEST STORY EVER TOLD

The story starts off with a loving God who left the wonders of his heavenly home so he could come down and share the good news of salvation with us. You'd think we would have welcomed him with open arms and exuberant hearts. Instead, on the night of his birth, an innkeeper wouldn't even give his parents a room for the night. His baby clothes were made from torn pieces of cloth that his mother used to keep him warm in the cold night. Not even she suspected that this precious child came to earth to die a violent death that would unlock the doors of heaven for all humankind.

I used to hear about Jesus when I went to church as a child, but I never understood that he was more than just a good man. In fact, he is the bridge that nullifies the great gulf my sin created between God and me. I am so grateful that Corwin took the risk to share his faith with me and encourage me follow in his footsteps. Thanks to his boldness, I surrendered to God, putting my full trust in him instead of following my own plans.

There are some things you should know about God. You need to know that he didn't just make this world, stick some people in it, and sit back on his throne with his arms crossed, waiting for us to get things right before we die. God isn't a passive observer. He wants to be intimately involved in every detail of your life. Not a moment goes by when you are not on his heart. He loves you completely and cares about all the challenges you face in this world.

Some of these challenges make it difficult to understand his love, but that's why Jesus came. He walked
in our shoes and subjected himself to the brutality of
humankind so we could know that God understands
our pain, our fears, and our struggles. He knows the
lure of temptation and the sting of rejection. He knows
the circumstances in your life that frustrate and infuri-
ate you. He knows the cruelty and abuse you have suffered at the hands of others. Jesus came to compensate
for all of that and more.

Jesus said, "The thief comes only to steal and kill
and destroy; I came that they may have life, and have
it abundantly" (John 10:10). What is the abundant life
that Christ came to give? It is a life of peace, purpose,
fulfillment, and hope. Think about these four things for
a minute. When you consider every goal for which you
strive in life, each one probably falls into one of these
categories: peace, purpose, fulfillment, and hope. Only
Christ can give you all of these things. So whether you
realize it or not, your ultimate goal is Christ!

## A RELATIONSHIP, NOT A RELIGION

The philosopher Blaise Pascal said, "There is a God-
shaped vacuum (or void) in the heart of every man
which cannot be filled by any created thing, but only by
God, the Creator, made known through Jesus." Most of
us try to fill that void with substitutes that bring only
temporary pleasure or worse, even more problems than
we had to begin with. As my story demonstrates, these

substitutes include money, power, success, pleasure, fame, and acceptance. But apart from knowing God and understanding his purpose for your life, such substitutes serve only to distract you from the true source of joy, purpose, identity, and hope.

True Christianity is not a religion. It's not about praying the right prayers, doing the proper rituals, or going through the motions. It's about a personal relationship with Jesus that cannot be practiced, chanted, or earned. Like any other relationship, it is simply lived. Jesus wants to be your Lord and Savior. But he also wants to be your friend, the type of friend who hopes and dreams with you, who listens to you when you're down.

As my story shows, sometimes God has to shatter our dreams so we can begin to dream his greater dreams for us. Our dreams are often self-centered. His dream is for us to use the gifts he has given us to impact the world. It is far more fulfilling than anything we could imagine. If you surrender to his will, he will help you become all that he created you to be.

Jesus said, "This is eternal life, that they may know you, the only true God, and Jesus Christ whom you have sent" (John 17:3). Until we surrender to Jesus, it's impossible to know him because of a dreaded word called "sin." Sin is more than breaking the Ten Commandments. It's outright rebellion against God. It causes us to shake our fist at God and say, "I'm doing things *my* way, not yours! I'm the captain of this ship. I will determine what is best for me. You can help me out, but only if you do it my way." We live in a world where rebellion against God is so common that we accept it as the norm. People sin all day, every day, and heartily encourage others to do the same. In fact, some look with disdain upon those who don't sin as they do.

Romans 3:23 reads, "For all have sinned and fall short of the glory of God." No one is immune. Scripture goes on to say, "The wages of sin is death." This is more than just physical death. It is eternal separation from God and his love. I cannot imagine a death worse than that!

## IF YOU WERE TO DIE TODAY, WOULD YOU GO TO HEAVEN?

When asked this question, most people say, "I hope so. I'm a good person. I've done a lot of good things for people. My grandma prayed for me, so I hope so…" What most people fail to realize is that we have more to go on than vague hopes. Jesus said, "For God so loved the world that he gave his only begotten son that whoever believes in him shall not perish but have eternal life" (John 3:16). This is more than hope. This is *help*, and we cannot get into heaven without divine help.

How did Jesus help us? Even though Corwin grew up in the church, he had a problem with Christ's crucifixion. He struggled with why it had to happen. He used to wonder, "If God is all-powerful, he should be able to do whatever he wants, right? Then why did Jesus have to suffer and die while his mother and all of his friends looked on helplessly?" Such questions went unanswered until Corwin heard the following story.

There was once a small-town judge who tried all of the community's cases. Everyone who committed a crime had to appear before this judge. He was adamant that anyone found guilty should receive the maximum penalty for the crime he or she committed. He believed that if you were willing to do the crime, then you should be willing to do *all* of the time. And so, one after another, as each person stood before him, the judge punished him or her to the full extent of the law.

Then one day, the judge's own son, whom he loved dearly, committed a grievous crime and had to stand before him in the courtroom. The news media came out, and all the townspeople wondered if the judge was going to stick to his convictions or be lenient on his son. With tears in his eyes, the judge brought down his gavel and gave his son the maximum sentence: death! Immediately afterward, though, he did something unprecedented. He stepped down from his podium, took off his robe, and declared, "And I am going to serve this sentence in my son's place."

This story is a good picture of what our heavenly Father has done for us through Jesus. What was our crime? Sin (Romans 3:23). What was our punishment? Death: spiritual separation from God (Romans 6:23). Even though, we deserved to be punished, God, the Judge of the universe, put on human flesh and came down to take the punishment for us (Romans 5:8). This is why the crucifixion could not be avoided. It wasn't a sign of God's weakness; it was the ultimate symbol of his power. He was punished to the full extent of the law so you and I would not have to be.

As you probably know, Jesus didn't just die on the cross. Three days later, over five hundred people, including his closest friends, saw him alive and well. That's why no one could silence them afterward. They saw the resurrected Savior with their own eyes, and they became an unstoppable force proclaiming this message of hope. Not even the threat of death could deter these bold men from going from city to city proclaiming the good news that Jesus was alive. That's because they knew that Jesus had just defeated death!

Jesus said "I am the way, and the truth, and the life; no one comes to the Father but through me" (John 14:6). *Wow! How could he make such a "narrow minded" statement?* you might wonder. It's because Jesus was the only one who died for our sins, and he was the only one *qualified* to die for our sins. That's why Acts 4:12 reads, "And there is salvation in no one else; for there is no other name under heaven that has been given among men by which we must be saved."

## IT'S YOUR CHOICE

Now that you have this information, I want to encourage you to do the same thing I did years ago that finally gave me the fulfillment I had been looking for. It's really quite simple. John 1:12 says, "But as many as received Him, to them He gave the right to become children of God, even to those who believe in His name." God gave us the gift of eternal life through his Son, but you can't receive that gift until you believe in your heart that Christ is the Son of God.

But *saving* belief is more than having head knowledge about Christ; it is a *heart commitment* to him that is an act of your will. I once heard a story about a man who strung a tightrope across Niagara Falls and then prepared to walk across it. A crowd gathered on the cliffside to watch. At first, they were horrified as they watched him struggle against the strong winds and the blinding mist that rose up from the waters below. But their horror turned to cheers as they watched him make it across and back successfully.

Then the man asked the crowd a question. "Do you *believe* I can walk across this rope while pushing a wheelbarrow?" They all cheered with one voice, "Yes!" So he took a wheelbarrow and pushed it back and forth successfully. More cheers rose up from the crowd. Then the man asked another question. "Do you *believe* I can walk across this rope with a person riding inside the wheelbarrow?" By this time, the crowd was giddy with excitement. "Yes, we *believe* you can do it!" they all said in unison.

Now imagine if you were one of the people in the crowd and the man turned to you, pointed to the wheelbarrow, and said, "Climb in." Would you do it? I think you'll agree that doing so would demonstrate a very different and more costly kind of belief. But this is exactly the sort of belief that God requires of us. Most people are willing to cheer Jesus from the cliffside, "You da man, Jesus!" But how many of us are willing to put our faith to the test and step into the wheelbarrow? Then and only then can you say you truly believe.

Though it may seem scary at first, you will soon learn that putting your life in Jesus's trustworthy hands is the safest thing you can do.

"For by grace you have been saved through faith; and that not of yourselves, it is the gift of God; not as a result of works, so that no one can boast" (Ephesians 2:8–9). This verse makes it very clear that you and I cannot work our way into heaven by being good people or simply identifying ourselves with the "right" crowd. The greatest need we have is forgiveness, and Jesus is the only one who can give it.

## IT ALL BEGINS WITH A SIMPLE PRAYER

If you desire to know and have peace with God, it starts by stepping into that "wheelbarrow" and trusting him with your life. I invite you to pray a simple prayer. It's similar to the one that I prayed on the day I became a Christian. This decision was the beginning of a journey of faith that transformed every aspect of my life. There is nothing magical about the words in and of themselves. But when prayed with a sincere heart, a miracle will take place.

> Lord Jesus, I need you and I want to know you personally. I thank you for dying on the cross for my sins. I want to accept your free gift of forgiveness. As an act of faith, I want to step into the wheelbarrow and trust you with my life and my soul, so I open the door of my heart and invite you to come into my life to be my Lord and Savior. I know that

I can never earn my salvation or be good enough to
deserve it, so I humble myself before you and simply proclaim that I believe.

If you have prayed this prayer, I want to be the first
to welcome you into God's family! It has been my
pleasure to introduce you to the greatest man I have
ever known. He is my Lord and my God, Jesus Christ!
Please know that God desires to give you a beautiful
hope just like he gave me. I want to encourage you
to find a good Bible-based church where the love of
Christ is displayed in the humility of his followers. If
for any reason you're hesitant to attend church because
you think you will not be accepted due to the circumstances surrounding your life, don't let that stop you.
Remember, none of us is perfect, so we should always
look to the ultimate example we see in the life of the
only perfect one who has ever walked this earth, Jesus.
He wants us to come to him just as we are, and when
we do, *he* will give us the power to change our lives. So
when you find a church that teaches the truth of the
Bible, welcomes you in spite of your faults, and helps
you to become more like Jesus, *this* is a church that is
showing the true love of Christ. My prayer is that God
will lead you to just the right place.

Don't try to go it alone like I did in college. Surround yourself with people who desire to walk in the
hope that only God can give. They will give you the
support you need to stand strong in a culture that is
diametrically opposed to God's ways. The encouragement and accountability these relationships can offer

will help you endure challenging times and live a life of victory instead of defeat.

---

If anything I have shared has impacted you in some way, I would love to hear about it! You can contact me through www.UnfavorableOdds.com. God bless you!

# TWENTY-FOUR

# SEVEN STEPS FROM PAIN TO PURPOSE

## 1. ACKNOWLEDGE THE PAIN

For many years of my life, I refused to acknowledge that I had been wounded by my circumstances while growing up. Instead, I suppressed the pain and pretended that nothing was wrong. Yet underneath the façade, all the pain still remained. It eventually surfaced as bitterness, insecurities, and low self-esteem. It wasn't until I acknowledged the hurt that I was able to begin the healing process.

Challenge:

A.  Honestly answer these questions:

> What are some of the hurtful things from your past that still bring pain to you today?

> How has this pain affected your past and current decisions?

Do you use being wronged as an excuse for how you live today?

What are some potential consequences for not dealing with the pain of the past?

B. Starting today, no longer allow the pain of the past to remain in the secrecy of the dark. Bring it to light by talking to God first, then to a trusted friend, counselor, or family member.

## 2. RECOGNIZE YOUR OWN MISTAKES

Every single one of us at one time or another has made poor choices. Whether it happened as a direct result of the pain someone else caused us or not, ultimately *we* will be held responsible for our own actions. Until we come to recognize our own imperfections and begin to take responsibility for them, we will not be able to experience true emotional, spiritual, and in some cases physical health.

### Challenge:

A. On a sheet of paper, list the areas of your life where you are making poor choices as a result of past pain. Take some time and prayerfully think through this step.

B. Ask God to forgive you for the wrong choices you've made.

C.  If you are a child of God, according to John 1:12, then accept his forgiveness. He has wiped your slate clean. (1 John 1:9)

## 3. FORGIVE OTHERS

If we don't forgive others, it is impossible for us to heal. I've heard someone say, "Not forgiving someone is like drinking poison and expecting the other person to die." When we refuse to forgive, we are only hurting ourselves. Forgiving doesn't mean that we forget. It means that we choose not to seek revenge or reciprocity. If you are currently experiencing abuse from someone, it is important for you to have boundaries in such situations. Please seek help from a pastor, a counselor, or someone who is trustworthy.

## Challenge:

A.  This might be difficult, but ask God to give you the strength. Identify the wrongs that have been done to you. List all of the people you *need* to forgive.

B.  Make the choice to give up your right to "pay them back" for what they have done. This doesn't mean that the feelings of anger will go away immediately. When the painful thoughts come to mind, you will need to remind yourself to forgive again.

C.  Begin to pray for the people on your list and ask God to give you the divine strength you will need to forgive over and over again. Remember, forgiving others doesn't mean *they* will change. Forgiveness is for *you*.

## 4. REDISCOVER THE TRUE YOU

Will the real me please stand up! Who are you? What are your likes, dislikes, dreams, passions, concerns, and goals? Now ask yourself if your answers are based on other people's opinions or your own *personal* convictions.

Who was I before I was wounded? What were the things that fascinated me in my younger years that I've since moved away from? What would I do if I had no concern about what other people thought of me? The truth is that some of us have dreams that we've never even shared with others because we are afraid of their response. Others of us have had our dreams shot down so many times that we've boxed them up and put them away on a shelf.

In order for us to be truly fulfilled in life, we must be true to who we really are, putting aside the actions and expectations of others and taking into consideration our own gifts, talents, and passions. We have been created as unique individuals with a variety of abilities and interests.

## Challenge:

A. Write out your definition of the true you. For what purpose do you perceive you were created? If you need help in identifying the true you, ask trusted friends about the uniqueness they see in you.

B. What steps can you take to begin living up to the true you without neglecting the relational and financial needs of your family? Remember, you may need to take baby steps, depending on what season of life you're in.

## 5. IDENTIFY YOUR STUMBLING BLOCKS

How has the pain you've experienced kept you from being all that you were created to be? For the the purpose of this exercise, I will define stumbling blocks as any negative attribute that can be used to describe a persons attitude, behavior or self-perception. Many times, these characteristics are developed as a result of how we are treated by others and can show up in the forms of low self-image, addictive behavior and fearfulness, to name a few. For example, has something someone said damaged your self-esteem, making it difficult for you to believe that you can succeed? Has neglect or abuse left you with the need to earn the approval of others instead of following your God-given passions and dreams? Has being abandoned by a parent left you unable to commit to and have genuine loving relationships? As you ponder these questions, some other stumbling blocks may come to mind.

Don't let your past pain prevent you from thriving in your relationships or careers. You don't have to be bogged down by those stumbling blocks. There is so much more to life than what you are experiencing!

Challenge:

A. Write down the stumbling blocks you have experienced in your life.

B. What belief patterns have you developed as a way of coping with your pain? (i.e. I will never succeed, nobody loves me, I have no value, I am a bad person, etc.) As a maturing adult, evaluate whether your belief system is healthy or needs to be discarded.

C. Relationally, what steps can you take to move toward developing healthy friendships and/or committing to a loving relationship? Biblical counseling can accelerate your understanding and give you a plan of action concerning healthy relationships.

## 6. TURN YOUR STUMBLING BLOCKS INTO STEPPING STONES

Focus on the positives. Your difficult circumstances in life are not meant to destroy you but rather to give you experiences that will make you stronger. This will enable you to fulfill the purpose for which you were created. As I look through my life, I see how quite a few things I thought were negative turned out to be blessings in disguise. The very things that were difficult for me ended up shaping my character and actually helped me to be more successful in my journey.

Challenge:

A. Write down some ways your circumstances may have made you a better person. Are you stronger, more innovative, or more compassionate? Have your circumstances given you a passion to help others in some way?

B. When you look at the real you, how can the strengths and character you've developed as a result of your challenges help you to be more successful as you pursue God's unique purpose for your life? (i.e. Your lack of finances may have given you a heart to help the poor or the need to be creative, which could be used to start your own business. The lack of love you received could foster the desire to encourage others. Your difficult childhood may have given you tough skin to thrive in the business world, etc.)

## 7. IF AT ALL POSSIBLE, RECONCILE

All of us have been hurt by someone at some point in our lives. In some cases it is impossible to reconcile with that person because of safety concerns, death, or other reasons. Each person has to assess his or her own situation. Just remember, we can still forgive without reconciling. Yet in most cases, reconciliation is an important step to healing and wholeness.

If you are wondering whether you are ready to reconcile, keep this in mind: If you take pleasure in the thought of confronting someone who has hurt you and your motive is payback, perhaps you are *not* ready. If the thought is coupled with a true desire to let go of the chains that have held you captive, then perhaps you *are*.

If you find yourself ready to reconcile, I encourage you to do so. However, please let me share some things that have been helpful to me as I sought to reconcile with my father.

## DO EVERYTHING TO AVOID ...

- Placing expectations on the other person.
- Speaking in a condemning tone.
- Disrespecting the other person (name-calling, etc.).
- Allowing the conversation to escalate into an argument. It takes two to argue.
- The fear of speaking the truth in love.
- The fear of asking the tough questions.

## DO ...

- Remember timing is everything.
- Make sure your heart and motives are right before your conversation.
- Pray and have others praying for you.
- Recognize any wrong action of your own.
- Prepare what you would like to discuss beforehand so you will be sure to cover the items that are most important.

- Listen to what the other person has to say, as long as it is not abusive. If you need to walk away, do so.

- Be open to understanding what the other person was going through during the time of the incident(s).

- Speak respectfully yet truthfully in terms of how the other person's actions affected you.

- Offer your forgiveness.

- Communicate your desires for how you would like the relationship to look in the future.

- Say all that you need to say and give the other person the opportunity to respond.

- Be ready to walk away with a clear conscience, no matter how the other person responds. You have done all that you can do.

Some of you will have positive experiences, and others will not. But no matter what the outcome, you can rest in the comfort that you did everything possible to right a wrong relationship. You will be able to walk away with a sense of peace and closure, leaving behind a painful past and focusing on a future of purpose.